ISEE Lower Level Practice Tests

ISEE Lower Level Practice Tests

Three Full-Length Verbal and Quantitative
Mock Tests with Detailed Answer Explanations

ANTHEM PRESS

Anthem Press
An imprint of Wimbledon Publishing Company
www.anthempress.com

This edition first published in UK and USA 2023
by ANTHEM PRESS
75–76 Blackfriars Road, London SE1 8HA, UK
or PO Box 9779, London SW19 7ZG, UK
and
244 Madison Ave #116, New York, NY 10016, USA

© Accel Learning LLC www.accellearning.com 2023

ISEE is not involved in the publication of this book and does not
endorse or sponsor this work.

British Library Cataloguing-in-Publication Data
A catalogue record for this book is available from the British Library.

Library of Congress Control Number: 2023936664
A catalog record for this book has been requested.

ISBN-13: 978-1-83998-980-3 (Pbk)
ISBN-10: 1-83998-980-7 (Pbk)

This title is also available as an e-book.

Contents

ISEE Overview

About ISEE

What is the ISEE?

What is ISEE? The Independent School Entrance Examination (ISEE) is an exam created and administered by the Educational Records Bureau (ERB). It tests students' individual academic achievements and reasoning skills as a basis for admission to private schools in the United States and internationally. The ISEE is the admission test of choice for many independent schools throughout the country and abroad.

The ISEE has five sections (in order of testing): Verbal Reasoning, Quantitative Reasoning, Reading Comprehension and Vocabulary, Mathematics Achievement, and an Essay which is written by the student in response to a given writing prompt. Each section is designed to tap into a unique aspect of a student's preparation for academic work. The first four sections consist entirely of multiple-choice questions.

How does a student arrange to take the ISEE?

Students may take the ISEE in one of the following ways:

1. The ISEE is given at individual school test sites at a wide variety of schools throughout the country and abroad and on a number of test dates.

2. The ISEE can also be given at the ERB office in New York and at offices in other parts of the country, visit: www.erblearn.org for more details.

What types of questions are on the ISEE?

The first four sections are composed of multiple-choice questions. The fifth section, the essay, is not scored but requires the student to respond to a preselected writing prompt.

The first two sections, **Verbal Reasoning** and **Quantitative Reasoning**, measure the applicant's reasoning ability.

The **Verbal Reasoning** test consists of two types of items: vocabulary and sentence completion.

At the Lower Level, the **Quantitative Reasoning** test consists of word problems.

The next two sections, **Reading Comprehension and Vocabulary** and **Mathematics Achievement**, measure the applicant's ability to correctly answer curriculum-based concepts that are appropriate at that grade level.

In order to determine a student's reading comprehension skills, in the Reading Comprehension and Vocabulary section, the student is asked to read a passage and then answer items specific to that passage.

Mathematics Achievement items conform to national mathematics standards and ask the student to identify the problem and find a solution to a problem. The items require one or more steps in calculating the answer.

The **Essay** is written by the student in response to a writing "prompt" or topic that is grade-level appropriate. The prompts rotate throughout the testing season. They are designed to prompt a student to write an informed essay on a particular topic.

The table below gives a quick snapshot of the questions in the ISEE.

Test Section	Questions	Time	Details
Verbal Reasoning	40–34	20 minutes	Tests vocabulary and reasoning abilities Synonym section focuses on word recognition Sentence Completion section measures students' knowledge of words and their function Use context clues to decide which word best fits the sentence
Quantitative Reasoning	38–37	35 minutes	Tests mathematical synthesis, skill, comprehension, and logical reasoning Quantitative Reasoning problems are higher-order thinking problems Interpreting data Solving application problems Estimating Recognizing patterns Solving nonroutine problems
Reading Comprehension and Vocabulary	36–25	35–25 minutes	Tests reading ability through six to eight passages, depending on the ISEE test level. Each passage is followed by at least four text-related questions
Mathematics Achievement	47–30	40–30 minutes	Correlates with common mathematics curriculum taught in schools Students may NOT use calculators on the ISEE
Essay	1	30 minutes	Students' essays must be in response to a provided prompt Students' essays are sent to each school that receives the ISEE score report Essays are NOT SCORED, but are instead evaluated individually by each school The ISEE essay section is intended for students to demonstrate their writing abilities

How will this book help me?

This book is structured just like the real ISEE. As you practice the tests given in this book, it will help you with:

- Build confidence.
- Get clarity on the topics.
- Build knowledge about the ISEE.
- Understand your strengths and weaknesses.
- Become familiar with the test layout, structure, and level of difficulty.

ISEE Test Taking

Why should one take the ISEE?

The school you are applying to has requested ISEE scores as part of the overall admissions process. By requiring an admission test for all students entering the same grade, the school can view one common item of all applicants. The school looks at many items in conjunction with the ISEE scores, including your application, your current school records, and possibly an interview. All components of the admission process, including the ISEE scores, help the school, you, and your family determine the best school match for you.

How many times can I take the ISEE?

The ISEE may be taken only when making a formal application to a school(s). You may take the ISEE only once per admission season, and you may not take the ISEE for practice.

What can I expect at the test site on the day of the test?

Students will present their verification letter or identification to be checked in upon arrival. They will be directed to the testing room. They will be provided with the testing material and other supplies. Although test administrators may not discuss test questions during the test, they give clear test directions, and you are encouraged to ask for clarification, if necessary, before beginning each section of the test.

Are there any scheduled breaks during the test?

There are two breaks—one following the Quantitative Reasoning section and another following the Mathematics Achievement section. Each break is 5 minutes long.

What materials do I need to bring to the actual ISEE?

Students should bring four #2 pencils and two pens with either blue or black ink. Students may choose to use erasable ink.

Are there materials that are prohibited from using during the ISEE?

Scrap paper, calculators, smartwatches, rulers, protractors, compasses, dictionaries, and cell phones are NOT permitted during the actual test.

Is there penalty for a wrong answer? Can I guess?

There is no penalty for a wrong answer, but it is not advised to guess.

ISEE Results

What happens to my scores?

After you take the ISEE and your answer sheet is scored, ERB will send copies of the scores and the essay you wrote to the schools that you have chosen, within 7–10 business days. They will send a copy of your test scores (but not a copy of the essay) to your family.

How is the essay scored?

The essay is not scored. However, a copy is sent to the school(s) to which a student sends score reports as indicated on the registration. Evaluation is based on each individual school's criteria.

How soon will I receive my scores?

Students will receive the scores in 7–10 business days.

What is the raw score?

A raw score represents the number correct. If a student got 35 items correct—say on a test of 40 questions—then the raw score is simply 35.

What is the scaled score?

Scaled score is a raw score that has been converted to a different numerical scale, e.g., 200–800. The raw score scale ranges from 0 to maximum score, while the scaled score range consists of higher numbers with a somewhat arbitrary minimum and maximum score. The range of scaled scores on the ISEE is 760–940.

What is the percentile score?

A percentile score is a relative score compared to other independent school applicants who have applied to the same grade during the past three years.

The percentile ranking helps private schools compare a student's performance with others in their applicant cohorts. **The higher your percentile, the better your ISEE score.** For example, a 45th percentile ranking means that the student scored the same as or better than 45% of students in the last three years.

What is a stanine?

A stanine score is simply another scale and is based on percentile ranks. Percentile ranks range from 1 to 99, while stanines range from 1 to 9. In general, a stanine score of 1–3 is below average, 4–6 is average, and 7–9 is above average.

How will I know if I passed or failed?

Students do not pass or fail the ISEE. There is no cutoff point that determines pass/fail status or divides students into these two groups. There is no cutoff (or pass/fail) score recommended by ERB.

ISEE—Lower Level Exam-1

Introduction

The **Independent School Entrance Exam (ISEE Exam)** is a school entrance exam taken by students in grades 4–12 seeking admission into private schools and non-Catholic religious schools throughout the United States. The Lower Level ISEE Exam is for students currently in grades 4 and 5 who are candidates for admission to grades 5 and 6.

The ISEE is an admission test that has three levels: A Lower Level, Middle Level, and Upper Level. The Lower Level is for students currently in grades 4 and 5 who are candidates for admission to grades 5 and 6. The Middle Level is for students in grades 6 and 7 who are candidates for grades 7 and 8. The Upper Level is for students in grades 8–11 who are candidates for grades 9–12.

Summary

Who can take the test?	Students from grades 4 and 5			
When is the test conducted?	Students may register to take the ISEE one time in any or all of three testing seasons. The ISEE testing seasons are defined as Fall (August–November), Winter (December–March), and Spring/Summer (April–July)			
What is the format of the test?	All questions are multiple choice			
What is the medium of the test?	Paper based			
What are the topics covered in the test?	**Test Section**	**Questions**	**Time**	**Details**
	Verbal Reasoning	40–34	20 minutes	Tests vocabulary and reasoning abilities Synonym section focuses on word recognition Sentence Completion section measures students' knowledge of words and their function Use context clues to decide which word best fits the sentence
	Quantitative Reasoning	38–37	35 minutes	Tests mathematical synthesis, skill, comprehension, and logical reasoning Quantitative Reasoning problems are higher-order thinking problems Interpreting data Solving application problems Estimating Recognizing patterns Solving nonroutine problems

(Continued)

(Continued)

	Reading Comprehension and Vocabulary	36–25	35–25 minutes	Tests reading ability through six to eight passages, depending on the ISEE test level Each passage is followed by at least four text-related questions
	Mathematics Achievement	47–30	40–30 minutes	Correlates with common mathematics curriculum taught in schools Students may NOT use calculators on the ISEE
	Essay	1	30 minutes	Students' essays must be in response to a provided prompt Students' essays are sent to each school that receives the ISEE score report Essays are NOT SCORED, but are instead evaluated individually by each school The ISEE essay section is intended for students to demonstrate their writing abilities
How long is the test?	Depending on the level, the actual testing time is between **2 hours and 20 minutes to 2 hours and 40 minutes.**			

Verbal Reasoning

You have 20 minutes to answer the 34 questions in the Verbal Reasoning Section.

This section is divided into two parts that contain two different types of questions. As soon as you have completed Part I, answer the questions in Part II. You may write in your test booklet. For each answer you select, fill in the corresponding circle on your answer document.

Part I—Synonyms

Each question in Part I consists of a word in capital letters followed by four answer choices. Select the one word that is most nearly the same in meaning as the word in capital letters.

SAMPLE QUESTION:

CHARGE:

(A) release
(B) belittle
(C) accuse
(D) conspire

Sample Answer

A B ● D

Part II—Sentence Completion

Each question in Part II is made up of a sentence with one blank. Each blank indicates that a word or phrase is missing. The sentence is followed by four answer choices. Select the word or phrase that will best complete the meaning of the sentence as a whole.

SAMPLE QUESTIONS:

It rained so much that the streets were _____.

(A) flooded
(B) arid
(C) paved
(D) crowded

Sample Answer

● B C D

The house was so dirty that it took _____.

(A) less than 10 min to wash it
(B) four months to demolish it
(C) over a week to walk across it
(D) two days to clean it

A B C ●

Part I—Synonyms

Directions:

Select the word that is most nearly the same in meaning as the word in capital letters.

1. FIERY

   (A) burning (B) wet (C) dull (D) insignificant

2. DODGE

   (A) tackle (B) duck (C) face (D) hit

3. UPSET

   (A) maintain (B) cheer (C) distress (D) enchant

4. SPILL

   (A) contain (B) enclose (C) keep (D) leak

5. GLOW

   (A) douse (B) shine (C) dim (D) dark

6. PATCH

   (A) ignore (B) mend (C) destroy (D) throw

7. MODIFY

   (A) keep (B) restore (C) change (D) original

8. QUARREL

   (A) argue (B) compromise (C) agree (D) give way

9. BELATED

   (A) early (B) on time (C) advance (D) tardy

10. CAUTION

    (A) surprise (B) unknown (C) secret (D) warning

11. FOCUS

    (A) aim (B) confuse (C) raffle (D) random

12. NOTICE

    (A) overlook (B) ignore (C) observe (D) disregard

13. SEIZE

    (A) free (B) let go (C) catch (D) liberate

14. KIDDING

    (A) serious (B) teasing (C) factual (D) rationale

15. IMPECCABLE

    (A) perfect (B) imperfect (C) sinful (D) flaw

16. MEAN

    (A) despicable (B) kind (C) good (D) friendly

17. NOMINATE

    (A) reject (B) decline (C) leave (D) choose

Part II—Sentence Completion

Directions:

Select the word that best completes the sentence.

18. Everybody has _____ their crushes to prom.

    (A) asked out   (B) asked around   (C) backed up   (D) blew up

19. The couple _____ for directions.

    (A) asked out   (B) asked around   (C) backed up   (D) blew up

20. My boyfriend _____ me over my decision to decline the offer.

    (A) asked out   (B) asked around   (C) backed up   (D) blew up

21. The president declined the class representative's _____ to volunteer the class for the summer cleanup.

    (A) revenge   (B) decision   (C) motion   (D) act

22. We spend the holidays _____ and our favorite places are in Europe.

    (A) abroad   (B) aboard   (C) indoors   (D) at home

23. The sisters climbed _____ the ship and said goodbye to their hometown.

    (A) abroad   (B) aboard   (C) indoors   (D) at home

24. He decided to _____ the castle to experience the beauty of life outside.

    (A) keep   (B) dessert   (C) uphold   (D) desert

25. The _____ they served at dinner was out of this world.

    (A) dessert   (B) keep   (C) uphold   (D) desert

26. The country was a vast _____ .

    (A) dessert   (B) desert   (C) uphold   (D) keep

27. The truck will _____ if it crashes to the fence.

(A) break in   (B) break up   (C) blow up   (D) break out

28. He asked help to _____ the balloons before his brother gets home for the party.

(A) break in   (B) break up   (C) blow up   (D) break out

29. After the trip, she _____ into a rash.

(A) broke in   (B) broke up   (C) blew up   (D) broke out

30. It is impossible to trust a _____ person because you never know where their loyalty lies.

(A) fickle   (B) honest   (C) constant   (D) loyal

31. Her mother cannot bear to see her child in _____.

(A) agony   (B) joy   (C) triumph   (D) success

32. Tell me what's your _____ for being late this time?

(A) objective   (B) alibi   (C) goal   (D) direction

33. Your skin acts as a _____ that serves as one of the body's first lines of defense against harmful microbes.

(A) opening   (B) entry   (C) barrier   (D) gateway

34. Everybody wants to _____ global warming but not everybody helps to make it happen.

(A) continue   (B) progress   (C) develop   (D) cease

End of section.

If you have any time left, go over the questions in this section only.

Do not start the next section.

You have 35 minutes to answer the 38 questions in the Quantitative Reasoning Section.

Each question is followed by four suggested answers. Read each question and then decide which one of the four suggested answers is best.

Find the row of spaces on your document that has the same number as the question. In this row, mark the space having the same letter as the answer you have chosen. You may write in your test booklet.

EXAMPLE 1:

What is the value of the expression $(4 + 6) \div 2$?:

Sample Answer

A   B   ●   D

(A) 2
(B) 4
(C) 5
(D) 7

The correct answer is 5, so circle C is darkened.

EXAMPLE 2:

A square has an area of 25 cm². What is the length of one of its side?

A   ●   C   D

(A) 1 cm
(B) 5 cm
(C) 10 cm
(D) 25 cm

The correct answer is 5 cm, so circle B is darkened.

---

1. What will come in place of x in this series?

    11, 5, 4, 4.5, x, 15

    (A) 5 (B) 7 (C) 6 (D) 8

2. What approximate value will come in place of question mark (?) in this question?

    $\sqrt[4]{257} \times 27.05 - 5.02^2 = ?$

    (A) 88 (B) 72 (C) 83 (D) 93

3. A rectangle and its length and width are shown below.

    If the area of a rectangle is length × width, what is the area of the rectangle above?

    (A) 16 + 49 (B) 16 × 49 (C) 16 × 49 cm (D) 16 cm × 49 cm

4. Which is the largest fraction?

    (A) $\dfrac{10}{11}$ (B) $\dfrac{13}{18}$ (C) $\dfrac{7}{14}$ (D) $\dfrac{6}{9}$

5. Moriah has a drawer of socks with five different colors: purple, green, black, white, and pink. The probability of her choosing a white sock is 7 out of 21. Which combination of socks is possible?

    (A) 3 white socks and 7 other socks (B) 6 white socks and 14 other socks

    (C) 7 white socks and 14 other socks (D) 9 white socks and 21 other socks

6. Which is a value of x in the math equation $\dfrac{13}{x} \div \dfrac{1}{84} = 273$?

    (A) $\dfrac{1}{2}$ (B) 0.4 (C) 12 (D) 4

7. If 81 can be divided by both x and 3 without leaving a remainder, then 81 can also be divided by which of the following whole numbers without leaving a remainder?

    (A) $x \div 3$ (B) x^2 (C) $x + 3$ (D) $x \times 5$

8. If nine 3 cm³ unit cubes make up one side of a larger cube, how many unit cubes make up the entire larger cube?

    (A) 38 (B) 27 (C) 54 (D) 81

9. Use the diagram to answer the question.

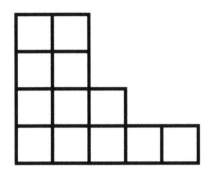

Which piece would complete the diagram to make a square?

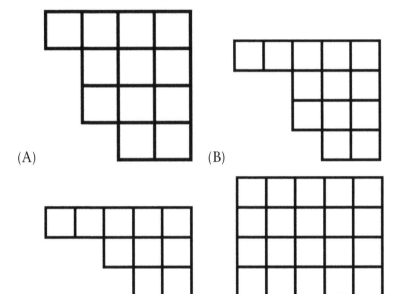

(A)   (B)

(C)   (D)

10. Use the questions below to answer the question.

$x - 20 = 25$

$y + 14 = 29$

What is the value of $x - y = ?$

(A) 35   (B) 60   (C) 30   (D) 40

11. At an enquiry office at Chicago Union Station a passenger was told, "A train for Santa Fe Station has left 25 minute ago," but after every 50 minutes a train leaves for Santa Fe Station. The next train will leave at 10:30 a.m. At what time was this information given to the passenger?

(A) 9.55 a.m.   (B) 10.05 a.m.   (C) 10.10 a.m.   (D) 10.25 a.m.

12. Sky starts from his office and walks 3 km toward North. He then turns right and walks 2 km and then turns right and walks 5 km, then he turns right and walks 2 km and finally he turns right and walks 2 km and turning to left starts walking straight. In which direction is he walking from the starting point?

(A) West   (B) North-East   (C) South-East   (D) South

13. Use the table to determine the rule.

Input ■	Output △
2	7
5	13
8	19
11	25
14	31

What is the rule for the function?

(A) (■ × 2) + 3 = △   (B) ■ × 3 = △   (C) (■ ÷ 2) + 1 = △   (D) ■ + 1 = △

14. The larger triangle below is divided into small triangles.

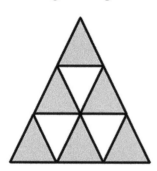

If the area of the larger triangle is 18 cm², what is the area of the shaded region in cm²?

(A) $\frac{1}{2}$ (B) 6   (C) 12   (D) 18

15. A survey of 360 students' favorite seasons is displayed in the circle graph shown.

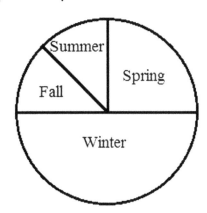

About what fraction of the students chose whether spring or winter as their favorite seasons?

(A) $\frac{3}{8}$ (B) $\frac{1}{2}$ (C) $\frac{3}{4}$ (D) $\frac{5}{8}$

16. Out of a total of 120 musicians in a club, 5% can play all the instruments—guitar, violin, and flute. It so happens that the number of musicians who can play any two and only two of the above instruments is 30. The number of musicians who can play the guitar alone is 40. What is the total number of those who can play violin alone or flute alone?

(A) 30   (B) 38   (C) 44   (D) 45

17. A child is looking for his father. He went 90 m in the East before turning to his right. He went 20 m before turning to his right again to look for his father at his uncle's place 30 m from this point. His father was not there. From here he went 100 m to the North before meeting his father in a street. How far did the son meet his father from the starting point?

(A) 80 m   (B) 100 m   (C) 140 m   (D) 260 m

18. In the following questions, three figures are similar in any way but the rest one is different from them. Find out the figures which are not different.

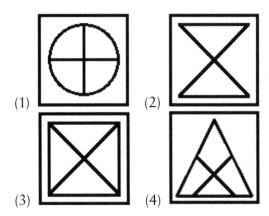

(A) (1), (2), and (3)   (B) (1), (3), and (4)   (C) (2), (3), and (4)   (D) none of the above

19. Line segment *AC* is 15 cm long.

A ————————————————|——— C
                              B

Point *B* is 2/5 of the way from point *A* to point *C*. What is the length of line segment *BC*?

(A) 3 cm   (B) 4.5 cm   (C) 6 cm   (D) 8.3 cm

20. Which of the following expressions has the same value as $169 \times \dfrac{7}{13}$?

(A) $\dfrac{7}{13}$ (B) 91   (C) $\dfrac{169 \times 7}{13}$ (D) $\dfrac{7}{169 \times 13}$

21. Nikolai conducted a survey of 10 random students at his school. He used the data to make the table below.

Student	Height (in)	Weight (lb)	Age (years)
1	65	132	13
2	52	75	10
3	56	90	12
4	61	122	11
5	61	103	15
6	67	152	14
7	59	101	13
8	54	82	12
9	58	93	10
10	60	142	11

What is the average weight of students in Nikolai's table?

(A) 109.20   (B) 108.89   (C) 16.22   (D) 136. 40

22. Use the number line to answer the question.

What is the sum of *A* and *B*?

(A) 4.1   (B) 2.05   (C) 3.3   (D) 0.8

23. The first five terms of a sequence are shown below:

3,000, 1,000, 333.33, 111.11, 37.04

What is the sixth term of this sequence?

(A) 15.02   (B) 14.99   (C) 12.35   (D) 16.46

24. Which story best fits the equation 76 ÷ 19 = 4?

(A) I have 76 books and my friend has 19 books. How many more books do I have?

(B) The total values of 19 pens are $76. What is the value of one pen?

(C) I have 76 boxes and 4 fit in each box. How many boxes do I need?

(D) None of these

25. If 3 = 0, 4 = 4, 5 = 8, 6 = 12, then 7 = ?

(A) 16   (B) 18   (C) 7   (D) 14

26. If 44 × 75 = 7,454, 34 × 65 = 6,453, 24 × 55 = 5,452, then 14 × 45 = ?

(A) 4,432   (B) 4,462   (C) 4,342   (D) 4,451

27. How many triangles are there in the given figure?

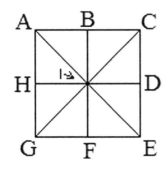

(A) 16   (B) 12   (C) 10   (D) 8

28. Find the missing link in the series?

$$\frac{1}{2}, \frac{3}{4}, \frac{5}{8}, \frac{7}{6}, \text{_____}, \frac{11}{64}$$

(A) $\frac{8}{24}$ (B) $\frac{9}{24}$ (C) $\frac{9}{32}$ (D) none

29. A boy earns thrice as much in the months of November and December as in the year. What part of the entire year's earning does he earn in November to December?

(A) $\frac{1}{16}$ (B) $\frac{3}{8}$ (C) $\frac{1}{4}$ (D) $\frac{7}{16}$

30. What is the average of 6 + 14 + 29 + 1 + 15?

(A) 46   (B) 65   (C) 13   (D) 17

31. Find the missing number 8 : 4 :: 26 : ?

(A) 9   (B) 7   (C) 5   (D) 13

32. A doctor weighted four new born babies. In his report, the doctor said baby A weighs less than baby B. Baby C weighs less than baby D. Baby B weighs less than baby D. Which baby weighs the least?

(A) A   (B) B   (C) C   (D) D

33. If $\sqrt{x} + \sqrt{49} = 8.2$, then x is equal to:

(A) 1.2   (B) 1.44   (C) 1.4   (D) 1.22

34. $2\dfrac{1}{17} \div \dfrac{7}{10} \times 1\dfrac{1}{33} = ?$

(A) $3\dfrac{1}{33}$ (B) $2\dfrac{1}{33}$ (C) $4\dfrac{1}{33}$ (D) $3\dfrac{1}{22}$

35. In the following series:

6 4 1 2 2 8 7 4 2 1 5 3 8 6 2 1 7 1 4 1 3 2 8 6

How many consecutive pairs of numbers have the difference of 2?

(A) 4   (B) 5   (C) 6   (D) 7

36. In a class of 39, Anos is 7 ranks ahead of Alex. If Alex's rank is 17 from the last, then what is the rank of Anos from the first?

(A) 14   (B) 17   (C) 15   (D) 16

37. Which diagram presents the associative property?

(A) $(\triangle + \square) = \triangle \, \square$ (B) $(\triangle \, \square) \times \odot = \triangle \times (\square \, \odot)$ (C) $\dfrac{\triangle}{\odot} = \dfrac{\odot}{\triangle}$ (D) $\odot\dfrac{\triangle}{\square} = \dfrac{\odot\triangle}{\odot\square}$

38. A pen costs $1.03 and Alex wants to purchase 398 pens. Which expression gives the best estimate of the total cost of Alex's purchase in dollars?

(A) $1 × 40   (B) $1 × 400   (C) $10 × 390   (D) $1.03 × 400

End of section.

If you have any time left, go over the questions in this section only.

Do not start the next section.

You have 25 minutes to answer the 25 questions in the Reading Comprehension and Vocabulary section.

Questions 1–6

An "extreme heat belt" reaching as far north as Chicago is taking shape, a corridor that cuts through the middle of the country and would affect more than 107 million people over the next 30 years, according to new data on the country's heat risks.

The report, released Monday by the nonprofit research group First Street Foundation, found that within a column of America's heartland stretching from Texas and Louisiana north to the Great Lakes, residents could experience heat index temperatures above 125 degrees Fahrenheit by 2053—conditions that are more commonly found in California's Death Valley or in parts of the Middle East.

The projections are part of First Street Foundation's new, <u>peer-reviewed</u> extreme heat model, which shows that most of the country will have upticks in the number of days with heat index temperatures above 100 degrees over the next 30 years as a result of climate change.

The heat index represents what a temperature feels like to the human body when humidity and air temperature are combined. It is commonly referred to as the "feels like" temperature.

"Everybody is affected by increasing heat, whether it be absolute increases in dangerous days or it's just a local hot day," said First Street Foundation's chief research officer, Jeremy Porter, a professor and the director of quantitative methods in social sciences at the City University of New York.

It has already been a <u>sweltering</u> summer for much of the U.S. and Europe. The National Oceanographic and Atmospheric Administration's latest monthly climate report, published Aug. 8, found that last month was the country's third-hottest July since record-keeping began nearly 130 years ago.

1. The main objective of this passage is

    (A) to convince readers that climate change is not true

    (B) to educate readers that Chicago is a hot state

    (C) to inform readers of the extreme heat belt forming as far north as Chicago

    (D) to teach readers how to measure heat index

2. In line 27, heat index is defined as

    (A) what a temperature feels like to the human body when humidity and air temperature are combined

    (B) temperatures above 100 degrees over the next 30 years as a result of climate change

    (C) conditions that are more commonly found in California's Death Valley or in parts of the Middle East

    (D) part of First Street Foundation's new, peer-reviewed extreme heat model

3. What does the underlined word in line 40 mean?

    (A) extremely cold   (B) frozen   (C) uncomfortably hot   (D) chilly

4. The passage gives enough information to answer which question?

    (A) Who invented heat index?

    (B) Which state is the hottest?

    (C) Is climate change true?

    (D) When was the country's third-hottest July since record-keeping began nearly 130 years ago?

5. When was the report stating that last month was the country's third-hottest July since record-keeping began nearly 130 years ago published?

   (A) August 8, 2022   (B) August 8   (C) August 8, 2021   (D) August 2022

6. What part of speech is the underlined word in line 20?

   (A) adjective   (B) adverb   (C) noun   (D) verb

Questions 7–12

Twenty people with diseased or damaged corneas had significant improvements in their vision after they received implants engineered out of protein from pigskin.

The patients, in Iran and India, all suffered from keratoconus, a condition in which the protective outer layer of the eye <u>progressively</u> thins and bulges outward. Fourteen of the patients were blind before they received the implant, but two years after the procedure, they had regained some or all of their vision. Three had perfect vision after the surgery.

The research team behind the technology published its findings Thursday in the journal *Nature Biotechnology*.

"We were surprised with the degree of vision improvement," said Neil Lagali, a professor of experimental ophthalmology at Linköping University in Sweden who co-authored the study.

Not all patients experienced the same degree of improvement, however. The 12 Iranian patients wound up with an average visual acuity of 20/58 with glasses; functional vision is defined as 20/40 or better with lenses.

Nonetheless, Dr. Marian Macsai, a clinical professor of ophthalmology at the University of Chicago who wasn't involved in the study, said the technology could be a game changer for those with keratoconus, which affects roughly 50 to 200 out of every 100,000 people. It might also have applications for other forms of corneal disease.

"The concept that we could have bioengineered corneas would be revolutionary," Macsai said. "It would potentially <u>eliminate</u> the risk of rejection and potentially make corneas available to patients worldwide."

7. The main objective of this passage is

   (A) to inform the readers of the implants engineered out of protein from pigskin and their efficacy

   (B) to educate the readers that pigskin will replace human eyes in the future

   (C) to tell readers that the implants were 100% effective to all eye conditions

   (D) to sell the implants to the readers

8. Which part of the eye was the implant for?

   (A) iris   (B) cornea   (C) sclera   (D) pupil

9. Where were the patients from the passage from?

   (A) Qatar and other parts of the Middle East   (B) USA and its territories

   (C) Southeast Asian countries   (D) Iran and India

10. What eye condition as the implant used for?

    (A) glaucoma   (B) nearsightedness   (C) presbyopia   (D) keratoconus

11. In line 7, which part of speech is the underlined word?

    (A) adjective   (B) adverb   (C) noun   (D) verb

12. In line 36, what does the underlined word mean?

    (A) qualify   (B) keep   (C) remove   (D) maintain

Questions 13–18

Plastic, then paper, now … pasta?

The humble straw that became a flashpoint in the broader battle over environmentalism continues to evolve. And while there's not as much fanfare, nonplastic straws are making inroads.

Companies are now making straws out of steel, silicone, glass, bamboo, hay, grass, seaweed, flour, pasta and, fittingly, straw. There has also been growing interest in continuing to create straws out of plastics, though companies have popped up that have developed straws made from biodegradable and compostable plastics.

Growth in the sale of these <u>alternative</u> straws has been significant. Kayla Via, the category manager of disposable drinkware and accessories at Clark Associates, a company that directs several national and international restaurant supply distributors, said eco-friendly and alternative straws constitute 22% of sales (in comparison to 65% for plastic and 13% for paper), but they are growing at by far the fastest rate, with 150% growth in 2022.

While traditional plastic straws are made of polypropylene, a growing number of straws and other single-use plastic products are being made of biodegradable or compostable plastics like polyhydroxyalkanoates (PHA) and polylactic acid (PLA). Straws made of such bioplastics are now highly represented in the market, offered by companies such as beyond GREEN and phade.

"It looks like, acts like, and behaves just like a traditional plastic straw," said Michael Winters, president and chief revenue officer of WinCup, the company that manufactures phade straws.

According to Yale Environment 360, bioplastics like PHA and PLA represent a $9 billion share of the $1.2 trillion plastic market. Ramani Narayan, distinguished professor in the department of chemical engineering and materials science at Michigan State University, said while traditional plastics have backbones made of very strong carbon-carbon bonds, bioplastics like PHA and PLA have a weaker ester backbone, which allows them to be consumed by microbes and thus degrade much more quickly than traditional plastics.

Still, Narayan worries that bioplastics often get overhyped.

"There is no magical solution, where you use it and <u>irrespective</u> of whether we manage it properly or you throw it away, that product will disappear and be removed from the environment. That doesn't exist," Narayan said of some of the plastic alternatives.

13. The main objective of this passage is

(A) that the straw industry has found ways to make straws more environment-friendly

(B) that straws will always be harmful to the environment

(C) to reintroduce straws to the community

(D) to sell straws to the readers

14. In line 3, what part of speech is the underlined word?

(A) noun   (B) verb   (C) adjective   (D) adverb

15. In line 9, what part of speech is the underlined word?

(A) noun   (B) verb   (C) adjective   (D) adverb

16. In line 14, what does the underlined word mean?

(A) substitute   (B) original   (C) only   (D) one

17. The passage gives enough information to answer which question?

(A) What are straws made up of now?   (B) Why it's okay to use plastic straws again?

(C) Who invented the first straw?   (D) How much is the current straw?

18. In line 51, what does the underlined word mean?

(A) including   (B) regardless   (C) according   (D) in line with

Questions 19–25

Professor Camilo Mora feels the impacts of climate change in his knees.

During a 2014 visit to his native Colombia, heavy rains caused the worst flooding his hometown had seen in decades and boosted the mosquito population. A mosquito bit Mora, transferring the chikungunya virus and making him a patient during an unprecedented outbreak in the region.

His joints ache still today. He blames a warming world.

In a study published Monday, Mora and his colleagues at the University of Hawaii canvassed tens of thousands of studies to analyze the global impacts of climate change on infectious diseases that affect humans. They determined that nearly 220 infectious diseases —58% of the total studied—had become bigger threats because of climate hazards.

"Systems have been evolving for millions of years and now humans have come along and changed things," Mora said. "We are punching nature, but nature is punching us back."

The study, which ultimately analyzed more than 3,200 scientific works, is one of the most thorough examinations of climate change's overall impact on diseases worldwide.

"It's only in the recent past of infectious disease research that we really focus in on climate change as a driver of infectious disease," said Jessica Leibler, an environmental epidemiologist at the Boston University School of Public Health who wasn't involved in the research.

Fifty-eight percent "seems like a really high number," she said, "but it reflects the reality that infectious diseases are driven by what's going on in our environment."

19. The main objective of this passage is

(A) to enumerate the infectious diseases there are that affect humans

(B) to prove that climate change has no impact on infectious disease rate

(C) to discuss the impact of climate change on infectious diseases

(D) to highlight which infectious disease is deadlier

20. In line 5, what does the underlined word mean?

(A) hinder   (B) increase   (C) decrease   (D) lower

21. In line 5, what part of speech is the underlined word?

(A) noun   (B) adjective   (C) adverb   (D) verb

22. The passage gives enough information to answer which question?

(A) How much of the 220 infectious diseases were studied that became bigger threats because of climate hazards?

(B) When did climate change start?

(C) Who is responsible for the climate hazards?

(D) How painful is the side effect of contracting an infectious disease?

23. In line 8, what does the underlined word mean?

(A) common   (B) unknown   (C) expected   (D) routine

24. In line 8, what part of speech is the underlined word?

(A) noun   (B) verb   (C) adjective   (D) adverb

25. How much of the 220 infectious diseases were studied that became bigger threats because of climate hazards?

(A) 58%   (B) 100%   (C) 25%   (D) quarter

End of section.

If you have any time left, go over the questions in this section only.

Do not start the next section.

You have 30 minutes to answer the 30 questions in the Mathematics Achievement Section.

Each question is followed by four suggested answers. Read each question and then decide which one of the four suggested answers is best.

Find the row of spaces on your document that has the same number as the question. In this row, mark the space having the same letter as the answer you have chosen. You may write in your test booklet.

SAMPLE QUESTION:

Which of the numbers below is not a factor of 364?

(A) 13
(B) 20
(C) 26
(D) 91

The correct answer is 20, so circle B is darkened.

Sample Answer

A ● C D

---

1. Which function is between $\frac{3}{5}$ and $\frac{1}{2}$?

   (A) $\frac{1}{10}$ (B) $\frac{3}{10}$ (C) $\frac{4}{10}$ (D) $\frac{2}{5}$

2. Use the set of numbers shown to answer the question.

   {19, 38, 57, 76, 95, ...}

   Which describes this set of numbers?

   (A) prime numbers (B) multiples of 19 (C) even numbers (D) odd numbers

3. Which number is divisible by 7 with a remainder of 2?

   (A) 135 (B) 141 (C) 126 (D) 178

4. What is the name of a polygon with four sides and four right angles?

   (A) kite (B) rhombus (C) rectangle (D) pentagon

5. What is the division of 13.2 and 3.9?

   (A) 3.41 (B) 3.38 (C) 4.70 (D) 3.33

6. Shown below is a plan for a parking lot that a grocery store is building. All angles shown in the plan are 90°.

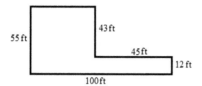

According to the grocery store's plan, what will be the perimeter of the parking lot? ($P = s + s + s + s + s + s$)

(A) 310 ft   (B) 322 ft   (C) 200 ft   (D) 160 ft

7. Use the number sequence to answer the question.
–7, –3, 1, _____, 9, 13, 17

(A) 2   (B) 3   (C) 4   (D) 5

8. The chart below shows Xenther's purchases at the store.

Item	Price of 1	Quantity
Jar of jelly	$4.59	2
Jar of peanut butter	$2.99	3
Loaf of bread	$1.39	4
Cold drinks can	$2.22	6

What is the total cost?

(A) between $8 and $16   (B) between $16 and $24   (C) between $24 and $32

(D) between $32 and $40

9. What is the mode of this set of data?

Time Spent for Watching TV (In Minutes)							
Week	Sunday	Monday	Tuesday	Wednesday	Thursday	Friday	Saturday
1	12	15	30	35	15	40	30
2	30	30	18	40	30	30	30
3	20	30	45	20	45	30	25

(A) 15   (B) 25   (C) 30   (D) 45

10. Look at the series: 24, 27, 30, _____, 36. What will be the number to fill the blank?
(A) 31   (B) 34   (C) 35   (D) 33

11. What is the value of the expression 6,770 – 361?

(A) 5,409   (B) 6,409   (C) 6,509   (D) 5,588

12. Which function is equivalent to 01.37?

(A) $\dfrac{137}{100}$ (B) $\dfrac{137}{1000}$ (C) $1\dfrac{37}{1000}$ (D) $\dfrac{37}{100}$

13. Jack asked 100 third graders at her school where they want to go on the next school field trip. The table shows the results.

Field Trip Location	Number of Votes
Art museum	17
Public library	13
Animal shelter	45
Police station	25

What fraction of the students wanted to go to either the animal shelter or the police station?

(A) $\dfrac{1}{2}$ (B) $\dfrac{7}{10}$ (C) $\dfrac{3}{4}$ (D) $\dfrac{4}{5}$

14. What is the standard form of eight thousand sixty-two multiplying by two hundred sixty-seven?

(A) 2,152,554   (B) 2,521,645   (C) 2,456,512   (D) 2,251,454

15. If the perimeter of a rectangle is 60 ft, which is the option below that can be used to determine the length of the rectangle?

($P = 2l + 2w$, where P = perimeter, l = length, and w = width)

(A) $l = 60 - w$ (B) $l = 90 - w$ (C) $l = 30 - w$ (D) $l = \dfrac{w}{90}$

16. Mrs. Morgan has 29 boxes of crayons. Each box contains 17 crayons. If Y represents the total number of crayons, which equation would tell her how many crayons she has?

(A) $29 \times 17 = Y$ (B) $Y + 29 = 17$ (C) $17 = \dfrac{Y}{29}$ (D) $Y = \dfrac{17}{29}$

17. If the area of a triangle is $\dfrac{1}{2} \times$ base $\times$ height, what is the area of the triangle ABC?

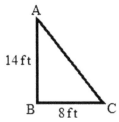

(A) 34 ft²   (B) 42 ft²   (C) 56 ft²   (D) 58 ft²

18. Which of the following expressions is equal to $19 \times \dfrac{33}{178}$?

    (A) $\dfrac{19 + 33}{178}$ (B) $\dfrac{630 - 18}{88 \times 2}$ (C) $\dfrac{19 \times 33}{178}$ (D) $\dfrac{627 \div 3}{33}$

19. Which of the following numbers is a multiple of 16?

    (A) 4   (B) 8   (C) 32   (D) 66

20. The graph shows the number of pies sold at a school bake sale.

Hours since Start of Scale	Pies Sold
1	☉ ☉
2	☉
3	☉ ☉ ☉ ☉
4	☉ ☉ ☉ ☉ ☉ ☉
5	☉ ☉ ☉

☉ = 5 pies sold

How many pies were sold at the bake sale?

(A) 16   (B) 90   (C) 160   (D) 220

21. Mrs. Jordon is 5.11 ft tall. There are 12 in in 1 ft. How many inches tall is Mrs. Jordon?

    (A) 55.32   (B) 61.32   (C) 66.09   (D) 61.032

22. What is the value of the expression: 198 + 227 + 386 − 564?

    (A) 472   (B) 247   (C) 338   (D) 250

23. Use the number line to answer the question.

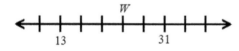

What number is represented by point W on the number line?

(A) 19   (B) 22   (C) 25   (D) 28

24. If (■ × 33) + 37 = 2,776, what number does ■ stands for?

(A) 2 (B) 95 (C) ±132 (D) 83

25. Polo asked 130 students what their favorite seasons were. The chart below shows her result.

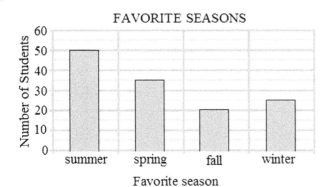

How many more students prefer summer than winter and fall combined?

(A) 20 (B) 5 (C) 25 (D) 35

26. What is the value of the expression?
(37 − 16 + 95 × 18) ÷ 3

(A) 356 (B) 877 (C) 757 (D) 577

27. In Mr. Paul's class of 30 students, 3 students are allergic to bees. If a bee flies into the classroom and stings a student at random, what is the probability that the student is allergic to the bee?

(A) $\dfrac{1}{100}$ (B) $\dfrac{1}{10}$ (C) $\dfrac{1}{3}$ (D) 3

28. If $7^x = \dfrac{1}{343}$, then the value of x = ?

(A) $\dfrac{1}{7}$ (B) 3 (C) −3 (D) $\dfrac{1}{3}$

29. Use the coordinate graph below.

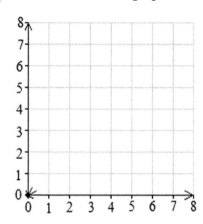

Alex plotted the following points on the coordinate graph:

Point A (2, 2); Point B (3, 5); Point D (5,3)

Where on the coordinate graph should he plot Point *C* so that the points form a rhombus with vertices *A*, *B*, *C*, and *D*, and sides *AB*, *BC*, *CD*, and *DA*?

(A) 5, 6   (B) 6, 6   (C) 6, 5   (D) 5, 3

30. Which of the following numbers is divisible by 9 without a remainder, but not by 6?

(A) 54   (B) 27   (C) 36   (D) 12

End of section.

If you have any time left, go over the questions in this section only.

Do not start the next section.

Essay Topic Sheet

The directions for the Essay portion of the ISEE are printed in the box below. Use the pre-lined pages on pages 37 and 38 for this part of the Practice Test.

You will have 30 minutes to plan and write an essay on the topic printed on the other side of this page. **Do not write on another topic. An essay on another topic is not acceptable.**

The essay is designed to give you an opportunity to show how well you can write. You should try to express your thoughts clearly. How well you write is much more important than how much you write, but you need to say enough for a reader to understand what you mean.

You will probably want to write more than a short paragraph. You should also be aware that a copy of your essay will be sent to each school that will be receiving your test results. You are to write only in the appropriate section of the answer sheet. Please write or print so that your writing may be read by someone who is not familiar with your handwriting.

You may make notes and plan your essay on the reverse side of the page. Allow enough time to copy the final form onto your answer sheet. You must copy the essay topic onto your answer sheet, in the box provided.

Please remember to write only the final draft of the essay on your answer sheet and to write it in blue or black pen. Again, you may use cursive writing or you may print. Only pages 37 and 38 will be sent to the schools.

Directions continue on the next page.

REMINDER: Please write this essay topic on the first few lines of your answer sheet.

Essay Topic

From the new English words, you have learned recently, which is your favorite? Why did you choose this word?

- Only write on this essay question
- Only pages 37 and 38 will be sent to the schools
- Only write in blue or black pen

NOTES

_____

_____

_____

_____

_____

_____

_____

_____

_____

_____

_____

_____

_____

_____

_____

_____

_____

_____

STUDENT NAME _____ GRADE APPLYING FOR _____

Use a blue or black ballpoint pen to write the final draft of your essay on this sheet.

You must write your essay topic in this space.

_____

_____

_____

Use specific details in your response

_____

_____

_____

_____

_____

_____

_____

_____

_____

_____

_____

_____

_____

_____

_____

_____

_____

_____

_____

_____

End of section.

If you have any time left, go over the questions in this section only.

ANSWER KEY

Verbal Reasoning

1.	A	7.	C	13.	C	19.	B	25.	A
2.	B	8.	A	14.	B	20.	C	26.	B
3.	C	9.	D	15.	A	21.	C	27.	C
4.	D	10.	D	16.	A	22.	A	28.	C
5.	B	11.	A	17.	D	23.	B	29.	D
6.	B	12.	C	18.	A	24.	D	30.	A

31.	A
32.	B
33.	C
34.	D

1. The correct answer is (A). Fiery means consisting of fire or burning strongly and brightly. It can also be used to describe a person having a passionate, quick-tempered nature.

2. The correct answer is (B). To dodge means to avoid (someone or something) by a sudden quick movement. Synonyms are dart, bolt, duck, and swerve.

3. The correct answer is (C). To upset someone is to make (someone) unhappy, disappointed, or worried. Synonyms are distress, trouble, disturb, and anger.

4. The correct answer is (D). To spill is to cause or allow (liquid) to flow over the edge of its container, especially unintentionally. It also means to reveal (confidential information) to someone. Synonyms are knock over, upset, disclose, and divulge.

5. The correct answer is (B). To glow means to give out steady light without flame like the tip of a cigarette. It can also mean to have an intense color and a slight shine. Synonyms are shine, radiate, and glimmer.

6. The correct answer is (B). To patch something is to mend or strengthen (fabric or an item of clothing) by putting a piece of material over a hole or weak point in it. Synonyms are mend, repair, cover, and sew.

7. The correct answer is (C). To modify is to make (someone or something) different; alter or modify. Synonyms are change, alter, adjust, and reform.

8. The correct answer is (A). To quarrel means to have a heated argument or disagreement. Synonyms are to argue, fight, and disagree.

9. The correct answer is (D). Belated means coming or happening later than should have been the case. Synonyms are late, overdue, delayed, and tardy.

10. The correct answer is (D). Caution is defined as care taken to avoid danger or mistakes. Synonyms are warning, awareness, and vigilance.

11. The correct answer is (A). Focus is an act of concentrating interest or activity on something. Synonyms are aim, emphasis, and priority.

12. The correct answer is (C). To notice means become aware of. Synonyms are to observe, perceive, and detect.

13. The correct answer is (C). To seize means to take hold of suddenly and forcibly. Synonyms are to catch, capture, and take.

14. The correct answer is (B). Kidding means playfully or teasingly deceptive.

15. The correct answer is (A). Impeccable means (of behavior, performance, or appearance) in accordance with the highest standards of propriety; faultless.

16. The correct answer is (A). To be mean means unkind, spiteful, or unfair.

17. The correct answer is (D). To nominate means to propose or formally enter as a candidate for election or for an honor or award. Synonyms are to choose, appoint, and recommend.

18. The correct answer is (A). The phrasal verb "ask out" means to invite on a date.

19. The correct answer is (B). To ask around means to ask many people the same question. Sample: "I <u>asked around,</u> but nobody has seen my wallet."

20. The correct answer is (C). To back someone up means to support someone. Sample: "My wife <u>backed</u> me <u>up</u> over my decision to quit my job."

21. The correct answer is (C). Motion means a formal proposal put to a legislature or committee. It also refers to the action or process of moving or being moved.

22. The correct answer is (A). Abroad means in or to a foreign country or countries. Sample: "We usually go abroad for a week in May."

23. The correct answer is (B). Aboard is a preposition which means on or into (a ship, aircraft, train, or other vehicle).

24. The correct answer is (D). To desert means to abandon (a person, cause, or organization) in a way considered disloyal or treacherous. Sample: "We feel our public representatives have deserted us."

25. The correct answer is (A). Dessert refers to the sweet course eaten at the end of a meal.

26. The correct answer is (B). Desert when referred to as a noun means a dry, barren area of land, especially one covered with sand, that is characteristically desolate, waterless, and without vegetation.

27. The correct answer is (C). To blow up means to explode. To blow something up also means to inflate or add air.

28. The correct answer is (C). To blow something up means to inflate or add air. To blow up also means to explode.

29. The correct answer is (D). To break out is develop a skin condition. It also means to escape from somewhere.

30. The correct answer is (A). Fickle means changing frequently, especially as regards one's loyalties, interests, or affection.

31. The correct answer is (A). Agnosy refers to extreme physical or mental suffering. Sample: "He crashed to the ground in agony."

32. The correct answer is (B). Alibi means an excuse intended to avoid blame. Sample: "She made up an alibi for why she was late."

33. The correct answer is (C). Barrier refers to a fence or other obstacle that prevents movement or access.

34. The correct answer is (D). To cease means to bring or come to an end. Sample: "The hostilities had ceased, and normal life was resumed."

Quantitative Reasoning

1. B	11. B	21. A	31. D
2. C	12. A	22. A	32. D
3. D	13. A	23. C	33. B
4. A	14. C	24. B	34. A
5. C	15. C	25. A	35. B
6. D	16. C	26. D	36. D
7. D	17. B	27. A	37. B
8. C	18. B	28. C	38. B
9. B	19. C	29. B	
10. C	20. C	30. B	

1. The correct answer is (B).

    The pattern is:

    $11 \times 0.5 - 0.5 = 5.5 - 0.5 = 5$

    $5 \times 1 - 1 = 5 - 1 = 4$

    $4 \times 1.5 - 1.5 = 6 - 1.5 = 4.5$

    $4.5 \times 2 - 2 = 9 - 2 = 7$

    $7 \times 2.5 - 2.5 = 17.5 - 2.5 = 15.$

2. The correct answer is (C).

    $\sqrt[4]{257} \times 27.05 - 5.02^2$

    $= \sqrt[4]{256} \times 27 - (5)^2$ (approx.)

    $= 4 \times 27 - 25 = 108 - 25 = 83$

3. The correct answer is (D). Here the sides are 16 cm and 49 cm therefore the area = 16 cm × 49 cm.

4. The correct answer is (A).

    L.C.M. of all denominators is: 198

    So, $\dfrac{10}{11} = \dfrac{10 \times 18}{11 \times 18} = \dfrac{180}{198} = 180$

    $\dfrac{13}{18} = \dfrac{10 \times 11}{11 \times 11} = \dfrac{143}{198} = 143$

    $\dfrac{7}{14} = \dfrac{1}{2} = \dfrac{1 \times 99}{2 \times 99} = \dfrac{99}{198} = 99$

    $\dfrac{6}{9} = \dfrac{2}{3} = \dfrac{2 \times 66}{3 \times 66} = \dfrac{132}{198} = 132$

    So, the largest fraction is $\dfrac{10}{11}$.

5. The correct answer is (C). In this question, it's clearly mentioned that Moriah chooses five different colored socks. Out of them she chooses seven white socks, and the rests are different four-color socks. So, 7 white socks and 14 other socks is true.

6. The correct answer is (D). $\dfrac{13}{x} \div \dfrac{1}{84} = 273 \Rightarrow \dfrac{13}{x} \times 84 = 273 \Rightarrow x = \dfrac{13 \times 84}{273} = 4.$

7. The correct answer is (D).

    We know $30 \div 5 = 6$; or $6 \times 5 = 30$.

    $\therefore x \times 5 = 6 \times 5$; or $x = 6$

    $\therefore x \times 5$ is true.

8. The correct answer is (C). We know a cube has six sides. If nine 3 cm³ unit cubes make up a side, then the number of total cubes is (6 × 9 number of cubes) = 54 cubes.

9. The correct answer is (B).

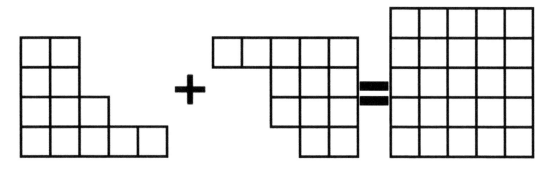

10. The correct answer is (C).

    $x - 20 = 25; \Rightarrow x = 25 + 20 = 45;$

    $y + 14 = 29; \Rightarrow y = 29 - 14 = 15;$

    $\therefore x - y = 45 - 15 = 30.$

11. The correct answer is (B).

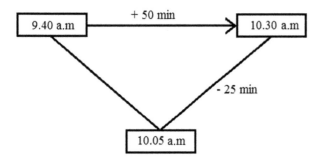

12. The correct answer is (A).

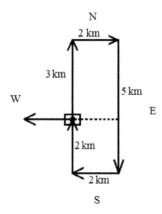

13. The correct answer is (A). $(2 \times 2) + 3 = 7$ and so on.

14. The correct answer is (C). Total area is 18 cm², the area of each small triangle 18/9 = 2 cm². Now there are six shaded small triangles, so the area of those shaded triangles = 6×2 cm² = 12 cm².

15. The correct answer is (C).

    Total students = 360

    Winter = 360 ÷ 2 = 180 Students

    Spring = 180 ÷ 2 = 90 Students

    Summer = 90 ÷ 2 = 45 Students

    $\therefore \dfrac{\text{Winter} + \text{Spring}}{360} = \dfrac{180 + 90}{360} = \dfrac{3}{4}$

16. The correct answer is (C).

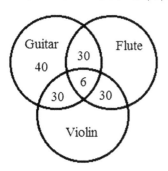

The number of musicians

who play guitar alone = 40. Six musicians can play all the three instruments. Thirty musicians can play any two and only two instruments. Thus, the total number of musicians who can play violin alone or flute alone = 120 – (40 + 36) = 120 – 76 = 44.

17. The correct answer is (B).

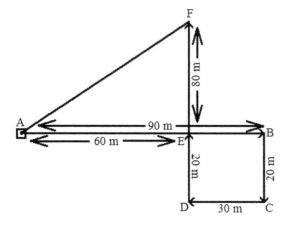

Required distance = AF

$(AF)^2 = (AE)^2 + (EF)^2$

or, $(AF)^2 = (60)^2 + (80)^2$

or, $(AF)^2 = 3,600 + 6,400$

or, $AF = \sqrt{10,000}$

$\Rightarrow AF = 100$ m.

18. The correct answer is (B). Except the figure (2), all the others are closed figures.

19. The correct answer is (C). $\dfrac{2 \times 15}{5}$ cm = 6 cm.

20. The correct answer is (C). The expression of $169 \times \dfrac{7}{13}$ is $\dfrac{169 \times 7}{13}$ and the simplification or answer is 91.

21. The correct answer is (A). Average weight =

$$\frac{132+75+90+122+103+152+101+82+93+142}{10} = \frac{1,092}{10} = 109.2.$$

22. The correct answer is (A). $\{(1.3 - 0.5) = 0.8\} = A$ and $\{(2.8 + 0.5 = 3.3\} = B$; $A + B = 0.8 + 3.3 = 4.1$.

23. The correct answer is (C). All the term of this sequence is divisible by 3. So $(37.04 \div 3) = 12.35$ (approx.)

24. The correct answer is (B). The total value of 19 pens is $76. What is the value of one pen? $\Rightarrow$ $76 \div 19 = 4$.

25. The correct answer is (A).

$3 \Rightarrow 4 \times 0 = 0$

$4 \Rightarrow 4 \times 1 = 4$

$5 \Rightarrow 4 \times 2 = 8$

$6 \Rightarrow 4 \times 3 = 12$

$7 \Rightarrow 4 \times 4 = 16$.

26. The correct answer is (D).

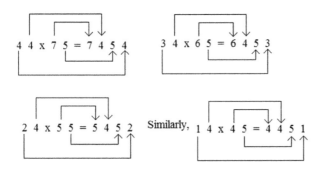

27. The correct answer is (A).

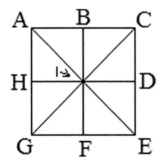

Triangles are: ABI, AHI, BCI, CDI, DFI, EFI, FGI, GHI, ACI, CEI, EGI, AGI, AEG, ACE, CEG, and ACG.

Thus, there are 16 triangles.

28. The correct answer is (C). The given number series is based on the following pattern: Add 2 to the numerator and multiply denominator by 2.

$$\frac{1+2}{2\times 2}=\frac{3}{4},$$

$$\frac{3+2}{4\times 2}=\frac{5}{8},$$

$$\frac{5+2}{8\times 2}=\frac{7}{16},$$

$$\frac{7+2}{6\times 2}=\frac{9}{32},$$

$$\frac{9+2}{32\times 2}=\frac{11}{64}.$$

So, $\frac{9}{32}$ is the correct answer.

29. The correct answer is (B). Let monthly income of the boy = $\$x$.

∴ Income in the month of November = $3x$

Total income of the entire year = $10x + 3x + 3x = 16x$

Part of income earned in the months of November and December

$$=\frac{6x}{16x}=\frac{3}{8}.$$

30. The correct answer is (B). The sum of the numbers = 6 + 14 + 29 + 1 + 15 = 65. Then the average $=\frac{65}{5}=13$.

31. The correct answer is (D). $\frac{8}{4}=\frac{26}{x}$, $x=\frac{26}{2}=13$

∴ The fourth number will be 13.

32. The correct answer is (D). D > B > A

D > C

∴ Child D weighs maximum.

33. The correct answer is (B). $\sqrt{x}+\sqrt{49}=8.2; \Rightarrow \sqrt{x}=8.2-7; \Rightarrow x=1.44$.

34. The correct answer is (A). $2\frac{1}{17}\div\frac{7}{10}\times 1\frac{1}{33}=\frac{35}{17}\times\frac{10}{7}\times\frac{34}{33}=\frac{100}{33}=3\frac{1}{33}$.

35. The correct answer is (B). Total five pairs, they are 6 – 4, 4 – 2, 5 – 3, 8 – 6, 8 – 6.

36. The correct answer is (D). Number of students in the class = 39

    Alex's rank from the last ⇒ 17th

    Anos's rank ahead of Alex ⇒ 7th

    or, Anos's rank from the last ⇒ 24th

    ∴ Anos's rank from the beginning 39 – 24 + 1 = 16th

    ∴ Therefore, correct answer will be (D).

37. The correct answer is (B). We know that a . (b . c) = (a . b) . c

38. The correct answer is (B). The near estimate of $1.03 is $1 and the near estimate of 398 is 400. Then = $1 × 400.

Reading Comprehension and Vocabulary

1. C	6. A	11. B	16. A	21. D
2. A	7. A	12. C	17. A	22. A
3. C	8. B	13. A	18. B	23. B
4. D	9. D	14. C	19. C	24. C
5. B	10. D	15. D	20. B	25. A

1. The correct answer is (C). The passage is from a news article regarding an "extreme heat belt" reaching as far north as Chicago taking shape. See line 1.

2. The correct answer is (A). See lines 27–30. The heat index represents what a temperature feels like to the human body when humidity and air temperature are combined.

3. The correct answer is (C). Sweltering means uncomfortably hot. Sample: "the sweltering afternoon heat"

4. The correct answer is (D). See lines 42–47. The National Oceanographic and Atmospheric Administration's latest monthly climate report, published Aug. 8, found that last month was the country's third-hottest July since record-keeping began nearly 130 years ago.

5. The correct answer is (B). See lines 42–47. The year when the report was published is not specified in the passage.

6. The correct answer is (A). Peer-reviewed is a two-word adjective which means something underwent quality control. A peer-reviewed publication is also sometimes referred to as a scholarly publication.

7. The correct answer is (A). The passage is a news article regarding how 20 people with diseased or damaged corneas had significant improvements in their vision after they received implants engineered out of protein from pigskin. See lines 1–4.

8. The correct answer is (B). See lines 1–4. The implant was engineered for those with diseased or damaged corneas.

9. The correct answer is (D). See line 5.

10. The correct answer is (D). See lines 5–6. The patients, in Iran and India, all suffered from keratoconus.

11. The correct answer is (B). Progressively is an adverb which means steadily, in stages. It modifies the verb "thins" in the sentence.

12. The correct answer is (C). Eliminate means completely remove or get rid of (something). In this sentence, the risk of injection is the object to remove.

13. The correct answer is (A). The passage is regarding an article discussing how companies are making alternative straws that are nonplastic and eco-friendly.

14. The correct answer is (C). Broader is an adjective in comparative degree which means having an ample distance from side to side; wider. It is describing the word battle.

15. The correct answer is (D). Fittingly is adverb which means in a way that is suitable or appropriate under the circumstances.

16. The correct answer is (A). Alternative means (of one or more things) available as another possibility.

17. The correct answer is (A). See lines 7–9.

18. The correct answer is (B). Irrespective means not taking (something) into account; regardless of. Sample: "Child benefit is paid irrespective of income levels."

19. The correct answer is (C). The passage is an article about studies proving that infectious diseases are driven by what's going on in our environment.

20. The correct answer is (B). Boosted is used as a past tense verb in the sentence which means to help or encourage (something) to increase or improve. The doer of the action is the heavy rains.

21. The correct answer is (D). Boosted is used as a past tense verb in the sentence which means to help or encourage (something) to increase or improve. The doer of the action is the heavy rains.

22. The correct answer is (A). See lines 16–19. They determined that nearly 220 infectious diseases—58% of the total studied—had become bigger threats because of climate hazards.

23. The correct answer is (B). Unprecedented is used as an adjective in this line which means never done or known before. It is describing the noun outbreak.

24. The correct answer is (C). Unprecedented is used as an adjective in this line which means never done or known before. It is describing the noun outbreak.

25. The correct answer is (A). See lines 16–19.

Mathematics Achievement

1. B	11. B	21. B
2. B	12. A	22. B
3. A	13. B	23. C
4. C	14. A	24. D
5. B	15. C	25. B
6. A	16. A	26. D
7. D	17. C	27. B
8. D	18. C	28. C
9. C	19. C	29. B
10. D	20. B	30. B

1. The correct answer is (B). The function between $\frac{3}{5}$ and $\frac{1}{2}$ is $= \frac{3}{5} \times \frac{1}{2} = \frac{3 \times 1}{5 \times 2} = \frac{3}{10}$

2. The correct answer is (B). The set of the multiples of 19 are 19, 38, 57, 76, 95, and so on.

3. The correct answer is (A). If we divide 135 by 7, the remainder will be 3.

4. The correct answer is (C). We know that a polygon with four sides and four right angles is called a rectangle.

5. The correct answer is (B). $13.2 \div 3.9 = \frac{13.2}{3.9} = \frac{132 \times 10}{3.9 \times 10} = \frac{\cancel{132}^{44}}{\cancel{39}_{13}} = \frac{44}{13} = 3.38.$

6. The correct answer is (A). Perimeter = Addition of all sides $\Rightarrow P = \{55 + 100 + 12 + 45 + 43 + (100 - 45)\}$ ft = 310 ft.

7. The correct answer is (D). {(−7 + 4) = −3}, {(−3 + 4) = 1}, {(1 + 4) = 5}, {(5 + 4) = 9}, {(9 + 4) = 13}, 13.

8. The correct answer is (D). ($4.59 × 2) + ($4.59 × 3) + ($4.59 × 4) + ($4.59 × 6) = $37.03.

9. The correct answer is (C). Thirty occurs maximum time, so the mode is 30.

10. The correct answer is (D). The pattern in this series is made by adding 3 to each number.

11. The correct answer is (B). 6,770 − 361 = 6,409.

12. The correct answer is (A). $01.37 = 1\dfrac{37}{100} = \dfrac{(100 \times 1) + 37}{100} = \dfrac{137}{100}$

13. The correct answer is (B). The total number of students who wanted to go to the animal shelter or police station is = 45 + 25 = 70. Total number of students = 100. Then the ratio is $\dfrac{7}{10}$.

14. The correct answer is (A). Eight thousand sixty-two (8,062) × Two hundred sixty-seven (267) = 2,152,554.

15. The correct answer is (C). Here $P = 2l + 2w$, therefore $2(l + w) = 60$, hence $l + w = 30$, so $l = 30 - w$.

16. The correct answer is (A). There are 29 boxes; each box has 17 crayons. ⇒ (29 × 17).

17. The correct answer is (C). We know Area = $\dfrac{1}{2} \times$ base $\times$ height = $\dfrac{1}{2} \times 8^4 \times 14 = 4 \times 14 = 56$ ft².

18. The correct answer is (C). $19 \times \dfrac{33}{178} = \dfrac{19 \times 33}{178}$.

19. The correct answer is (C). The multiple of 16 is 32.

20. The correct answer is (B). The total number of pies sold = 18 × 5 = 90.

21. The correct answer is (B). 1 ft = 12 in; ⇒ (5.11 ft × 12 in) = 61.32 in.

22. The correct answer is (B). 198 + 227 + 386 − 564 = 247.

23. The correct answer is (C). (13 + 3) = 16; (16 + 3) = 19; (19 + 3) = 22; (22 + 3) = 25; (25 + 3) = 28; (28 + 3) = 33, and so on. ⇒ 25 is the right answer.

24. The correct answer is (D). (■ × 33) + 37 = 2,776; Let ■ = x;

$(x \times 33) + 37 = 2,776$; $33x = 2,776 - 37$; $\Rightarrow x = \dfrac{2,739}{33} = 83$.

25. The correct answer is (B). The total number of students like summer = 50, winter = 25, a fall = 20. So five more students like summer than winter and fall combined.

26. The correct answer is (D). $(37 - 16 + 95 \times 18) \div 3 = (37 - 16 + 1,710) \div 3 = (37 + 1,710 - 16) \div 3 = (1,747 - 16) \div 3 = 1,731 \div 3 = 577$.

27. The correct answer is (B). Three students are allergic to bees; there are 30 students, then the probability of bee stinging an allergic student is $= \dfrac{3}{30} = \dfrac{1}{10}$.

28. The correct answer is (C). $7^x = \dfrac{1}{343} \Rightarrow 7^x = \dfrac{1}{7^{-3}} \Rightarrow 7^x = 7^{-3} \Rightarrow \Rightarrow x = -3$.

29. The correct answer is (B).

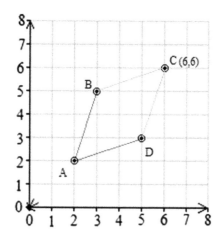

30. The correct answer is (B). Among the options only 27 is divided by 9. So, it is the answer.

Sample Essay Response

Among the words I have learned recently, my favorite is wonderstruck. It means being in awe or struck with wonder and admiration. It is such a strong word yet positive in meaning. Just like learning English, it left me wonderstruck.

People say English is a weird language. It is weird for many reasons such as when Americans spell the word color with a single vowel while the British add the letter "u". Both have the same meaning and are acceptable.

Without touching the topic of grammar rules, English itself is already unusual. English is weird in many ways not to mention the complex spelling rules and their fondness of idioms. English has more speech sounds than many languages and has unusually large sets of vowels. There are 11 vowels to be exact. According to the World Atlas of Language Structures, most spoken languages only have five to six vowel sounds. In addition to the large set of vowel sounds, it also has unusual consonant sounds such as the rule of "*th*". When you say "them" and "thought", both words are spelled with "*th*" but do not sound the same when pronounced.

Although English is strange, many aspire to learn the language. Personally, it is part of my curriculum at school so there was really no way of escaping English. I am glad that I learned English because of the opportunities it led me and relationships I was able to build using the language. These are what made me wonderstruck by English as language, and it is why it became my favorite word.

For the ISEE, the most commonly referenced score is the stanine score. Check out the four steps to calculating stanine scores.

Step 1: The Raw Score

The first step in scoring is calculating a raw score. This is quite simple.

Students receive one point for each correct answer and no points for incorrect answers or unanswered questions.

Tip: Because there is no score penalty for incorrect answers or unanswered questions, be sure to answer every single question! Answering all of the questions can only increase your chances of a higher score.

Step 2: The Scaled Score

Once a raw score has been calculated for each section, it is converted into a scaled score.

This conversion adjusts for the variation in difficulty between different tests. Thus, a lower raw score on a harder test could give you the same scaled score as a higher raw score on an easier test. This process is called equating.

The scaled score for each section ranges from 760 to 940.

Step 3: The Percentile Score

Next, the percentile score for each section is calculated.

Percentiles compare a student's scaled score to all other same-grade students from the past three years. This is important to understand because the ISEE is taken by students in a range of grades. The Upper Level ISEE, for instance, is taken by students applying to grades 9–12; however, the percentile score is based only on the performance of other students applying to the same grade. Thus, a student applying to 9th grade will not be compared to a student applying to 12th grade.

Here's an example to help understand percentile scores: scoring in the 40th percentile indicates that a student scored the same or higher than 40% of students in the same grade but lower than 59% of students.

Step 4: The Stanine Score

Finally, the percentile is converted into a stanine score.

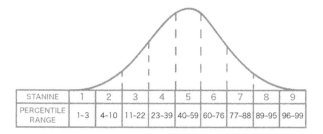

STANINE	1	2	3	4	5	6	7	8	9
PERCENTILE RANGE	1–3	4–10	11–22	23–39	40–59	60–76	77–88	89–95	96–99

Notice that the percentile ranges for the middle stanines of 4–6 are far larger than the ranges for the extreme stanines of 1, 2, 8, or 9. This means that most students taking the ISEE achieve scores in the middle ranges. Only the top 4% of all test takers receive a stanine of 9 on any given section, while 20% of students receive a stanine of 5.

So, what is a good ISEE score?

Stanine scores (which range from 1 to 9) are the most important and are the scores schools pay the most attention to. But what is a good score on the ISEE? A score of 5 or higher will be enough to put students in the running for most schools, although some elite private schools want applicants to have ISEE test results of 7 or higher.

Here's a sample ISEE Report

Candidate for Grade	8
ID Number	
Gender	Male
Date of Birth	4/8/2004
Phone Number	
Test Level/Form	Middle/0916
Date of Testing	11/30/2016
Tracking Number	201612010592103

Individual Student Report

The Test Profile below shows your total scores for each test. Refer to the enclosed brochure called *Understanding the Individual Student Report* to help you interpret the *Test Profile* and *Analysis*. Percentile Ranks and Stanines are derived from norms for applicants to independent schools.

TEST PROFILE

Section	Scaled Score (760 – 940)	Percentile Rank (1 – 99)	Stanine (1 – 9)	Stanine Analysis 1 2 3 4 5 6 7 8 9
Verbal Reasoning	895	90	8	V
Reading Comprehension	890	76	6	R
Quantitative Reasoning	894	81	7	Q
Mathematics Achievement	883	61	6	M

LEGEND: V = Verbal Reasoning R = Reading Comprehension Q = Quantitative Reasoning M = Mathematics Achievement

ANALYSIS

Section & Subsection	# of Questions	# Correct	Results for Each Question
Verbal Reasoning			
Synonyms	18	15	+++++++- ++++- ++- +
Single Word Response	17	16	+++++++++++- +++++
Quantitative Reasoning			
Word Problems	18	11	+++- - - +++- +++++- - -
Quantitative Comparisons	14	14	++++++++++++++
Reading Comprehension			
Main Idea	4	4	++++
Supporting Ideas	6	5	- +++++
Inference	6	5	+- ++++
Vocabulary	7	5	+++- +- +
Organization/Logic	4	4	++++
Tone/Style/Figurative Language	3	3	+++
Mathematics Achievement			
Whole Numbers	7	4	+- +++- -
Decimals, Percents, Fractions	9	5	++- - ++- - +
Algebraic Concepts	11	7	+++++- ++- - -
Geometry	4	2	+- +-
Measurement	5	4	++++-
Data Analysis and Probability	6	4	+++- +-

LEGEND: + = Correct   - = Incorrect   S = Skipped   N = Not Reached

The test was administered in the order reported in the analysis section; Verbal Reasoning, Quantitative Reasoning, Reading Comprehension, and Mathematics Achievement. Each section was divided into subsections, grouping similar types of questions. The Reading Comprehension subsection grouping does not represent the actual order of the test questions.

The above is a preliminary ISEE report. ERB reserves the right to amend this report before it is finalized. The report will be final no later than 20 business days. The final report will automatically be generated electronically.

ISEE—Lower Level Exam-2

Verbal Reasoning

You have 20 minutes to answer the 34 questions in the Verbal Reasoning Section.

This section is divided into two parts that contain two different types of questions. As soon as you have completed Part I, answer the questions in Part II. You may write in your test booklet. For each answer you select, fill in the corresponding circle on your answer document.

Part I—Synonyms

Each question in Part I consists of a word in capital letters followed by four answer choices. Select the one word that is most nearly the same in meaning as the word in capital letters.

SAMPLE QUESTION: Sample Answer

CHARGE: A   B   ●   D

(A) release
(B) belittle
(C) accuse
(D) conspire

Part II—Sentence Completion

Each question in Part II is made up of a sentence with one blank. Each blank indicates that a word or phrase is missing. The sentence is followed by four answer choices. Select the word or phrase that will best complete the meaning of the sentence as a whole.

SAMPLE QUESTIONS: Sample Answer

It rained so much that the streets were _____.   ●   B   C   D

(A) flooded
(B) arid
(C) paved
(D) crowded

The house was so dirty that it took _____.   A   B   C   ●

(A) less than 10 min to wash it
(B) four months to demolish it
(C) over a week to walk across it
(D) two days to clean it

Part I—Synonyms

Directions:

Select the word that is most nearly the same in meaning as the word in capital letters.

1. ACCEPTABLE

    (A) undesirable (B) satisfactory (C) unwelcome (D) insignificant

2. ACCOMPANY

    (A) leave (B) free (C) escort (D) enslave

3. ADVANTAGE

    (A) benefit (B) detriment (C) drawback (D) handicap

4. AMUSING

    (A) boring (B) solemn (C) discreet (D) entertaining

5. ANCIENT

    (A) new (B) recent (C) modern (D) old

6. ANIMATE

    (A) inhibit (B) inspire (C) depress (D) discourage

7. ANXIOUS

    (A) worried (B) carefree (C) unconcerned (D) nonchalant

8. ARGUE

    (A) quarrel (B) agree (C) compromise (D) give way

9. ARREST

    (A) release (B) start (C) apprehend (D) continue

10. ASHAMED

    (A) proud (B) unapologetic (C) pleased (D) embarrassed

11. ATTEMPT

    (A) give up (B) strive (C) aimless (D) random

12. BAGGAGE

    (A) vegetable (B) belongings (C) waste (D) vehicle

13. BASIC

    (A) secondary (B) unimportant (C) accessory (D) primary

14. BEHAVE

    (A) proper (B) mess (C) carefree (D) unprofessional

15. BELIEVE

    (A) doubt (B) argue (C) trust (D) disapprove

16. BET

    (A) doubt (B) risk (C) unsure (D) against

17. BLOCK

    (A) open (B) seal (C) spill (D) loosen

Part II—Sentence Completion

> **Directions:**
> Select the word that best completes the sentence.

18. He has been drinking _____ to their canceled engagement.

    (A) get over   (B) get behind   (C) get under   (D) get on top

19. _____ in the morning is always the hardest task of the day.

    (A) getting down   (B) getting under   (C) getting up   (D) getting close

20. Our proposal got _____ because of the copyright issue.

    (A) turned over   (B) turned up   (C) turned down   (D) turned back

21. Even if mom was late, I'm glad she decided to _____ at my graduation.

    (A) turn over   (B) turn up   (C) turn down   (D) turn back

22. There's no _____ now.

    (A) turning over   (B) turning up   (C) turning down   (D) turning back

23. Somebody _____ a cat and left it in the street.

    (A) ran up   (B) ran under   (C) ran after   (D) ran over

24. I will be waiting _____ you.

    (A) for   (B) in   (C) on   (D) over

25. Go straight _____ bed once homework is done.

    (A) for   (B) to   (C) of   (D) in

26. Throw your trash into the _____.

    (A) bean   (B) been   (C) bin   (D) ban

27. The properties on _____ almost never gets claimed back and are just left rotting.

(A) lien   (B) lean   (C) line   (D) lend

28. Dietitians recommend _____ meat to help combat heart disease and other conditions.

(A) lien   (B) lean   (C) line   (D) lend

29. She was _____ for her leadership.

(A) commented   (B) commanded   (C) committed   (D) commended

30. He got punished for _____ an irreversible error.

(A) committing   (B) commenting   (C) commanding   (D) commending

31. She got annoyed of people _____ on her sister's appearance.

(A) committing   (B) commanding   (C) commenting   (D) commending

32. She needed time to _____ after barely escaping a stalker.

(A) calm down   (B) calm on   (C) calm over   (D) calm in

33. If you give her time to think about your idea, she'll _____.

(A) come in   (B) come around   (C) come on   (D) come up

34. Everybody met to _____ the class presentation for the summer festival.

(A) come in   (B) come up with   (C) come on   (D) come over

End of section.

If you have any time left, go over the questions in this section only.

Do not start the next section.

You have 35 minutes to answer the 38 questions in the Quantitative Reasoning Section.

Each question is followed by four suggested answers. Read each question and then decide which one of the four suggested answers is best.

Find the row of spaces on your document that has the same number as the question. In this row, mark the space having the same letter as the answer you have chosen. You may write in your test booklet.

EXAMPLE 1:   Sample Answer

What is the value of the expression $(4 + 6) \div 2$?   A B ● D

(A) 2
(B) 4
(C) 5
(D) 7

The correct answer is 5, so circle C is darkened.

EXAMPLE 2:

A square has an area of 25 cm². What is the length of one of its side?   A ● C D

(A) 1 cm
(B) 5 cm
(C) 10 cm
(D) 25 cm

The correct answer is 5 cm, so circle B is darkened.

---

1. Look at this series:

12, 11, 13, 12, 14, 13

What number should come next?

(A) 10   (B) 16   (C) 13   (D) 15

2. Poppy has a drawer of socks with six different colors: purple, green, yellow, black, blue, and pink. The probability of her choosing a white sock is 9 out of 54. Which combination of socks is possible?

(A) 6 white socks and 15 other socks   (B) 9 white socks and 45 other socks   (C) 9 white socks and 54 other socks   (D) 7 white socks and 30 other socks

3. A square and its length are shown below.

29 cm

What is the half of perimeter of the square above?

(A) $(29 + 29)^2$ (B) $\dfrac{16 \times 49}{4}$ (C) $\dfrac{4 \times 29}{2}$ cm²   (D) $\dfrac{4 \times 29}{2}$ cm

4. Which is the lowest fraction?

(A) $2\dfrac{1}{2}$ (B) $\dfrac{1.3}{8}$ (C) $1\dfrac{2}{3}$ cm²   (D) $\dfrac{1}{10}$ cm

5. If P means ×, Q means ÷, R means +, and S means –, then what is the value of 154 Q 14 S 7 P 3 R 25?

(A) 35   (B) 15   (C) 42   (D) 57

6. If 56 can be divided by both x and 14 without leaving a remainder, then 126 can also be divided by which of the following whole numbers without leaving a remainder?

(A) $x \times 14$ (B) $x \div 14$ (C) x^2 (D) $x + 14$

7. Which signs and numbers should be interchanged so the given equation will be correct?

$(12 \div 6) + 3 \times 7 = 42$

(A) + and ×   (B) 6 and 7   (C) ÷ and +   (D) 12 and 3

8. Use the diagram to answer the question.

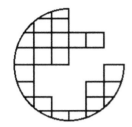

Which piece would complete the diagram to make a square?

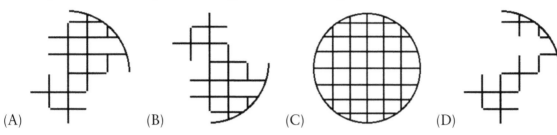

(A) (B) (C) (D)

9. Use the questions below to answer the question.

$2x - 5 = 45$

$3y + 13 = 112$

What is the value of $3x + 2y = ?$

(A) 159   (B) 112   (C) 45   (D) 99

10. A car runs 150 km on 15 L of fuel, how many kilometers will it run on 10 L of fuel?

(A) 100 km   (B) 10 km   (C) 95.20 km   (D) none of the above

11. Use the table to determine the rule.

Input Ø	Output ⊕
2	10
3	13
7	25
9	31
11	37

What is the rule for the function?

(A) Ø × 3 = ⊕   (B) (Ø ÷ 2) + 1 = ⊕   (C) (Ø × 3) + 4 = ⊕   (D) Ø + 1 = ⊕

12. The larger square below is divided into small squares.

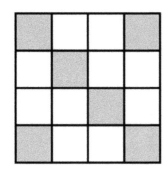

If the area of the larger triangle is 96 m², what is the area of the shaded region in m²?

(A) 36   (B) 60   (C) 54   (D) 18

13. Which of the following expressions has the same value as $605 \div \dfrac{15}{36} \times 12$?

(A) $\dfrac{605 \times 36 \times 12}{15}$ (B) $\dfrac{7}{13}$ (C) 91   (D) $\dfrac{605 \times 36}{15 \times 12}$

14. Use the number line to answer the question.

What is the value of $(A + B + C) \div 3$?

(A) 34   (B) 20   (C) 33   (D) 20.5

15. How many squares are there in the given figure?

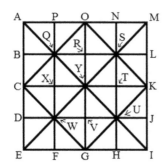

(A) 20   (B) 21   (C) 16   (D) 18

16. Find the missing number 18 : 12 :: 36 : ?

(A) 72   (B) 24   (C) 36   (D) 18

17. $\sqrt{y} + \sqrt{64} = 9.39$, then y is equal to:

(A) 2   (B) 1.39   (C) 0.99   (D) 1.93

18. What is the average of the following series?

11, 3, 9, 35, 16, 20

(A) 15.67 (B) 18.55 (C) 32 (D) 35

19. In a class of 80, Mia is two ranks ahead of Oscar. If Oscar's rank is 50 from the last, then what is the rank of Mia from the first?

(A) 50 (B) 35 (C) 37 (D) 52

20. What approximate value will come in place of question mark (?) in the following?

$\sqrt[4]{625} \div 5 - 2 + 14 = ?$

(A) 18.09 (B) 19 (C) 17 (D) 16

21. Which of the following set of signs should be used to replace "*" in the following?

25*2*6 = 4*11*0

(A) ×, −, ×, + (B) +, −, ×, + (C) ×, +, ×, − (D) ×, +, +, ×

22. Some equations are solved according to a specific method. Solve the unsolved equation following this method: If 10 − 3 = 12, 12 − 4 = 13, 14 − 5 = 14, then, 16 − 6 = ?

(A) 10 (B) 15 (C) 16 (D) 18

23. Simplify: [{12 + (7 × 4)} ÷ 4 + {(6 × 9)÷ 3}] ÷ 4.

(A) 14 (B) 28 (C) 7 (D) 9

24. Find the average of: 31 + 64 + 21 + 9 + 12 + 3.

(A) 13.34 (B) 23.33 (C) 30.55 (D) 20.01

25. The greatest common factor of 10, 25 is

(A) 10 (B) 25 (C) 5 (D) 1

26. If $60 \times A\% = 15$, then $A = ?$

(A) $A = 20$ (B) $A = 25$ (C) $A = 30$ (D) $A = 35$

27. Solve: 62.92 × 0.0736

(A) 4.360192 (B) 4.036192 (C) 3.046192 (D) 4.630912

28. Look at the series and find the next number: 2, 5, 8, 11, _____.

(A) 13 (B) 14 (C) 12 (D) 15

29. Andrew finishes his work in 15 days while Bruno takes 10 days. How many days will the same work be done if they work together?

(A) 12 days   (B) 13 days   (C) 6 days   (D) 1 day

30.

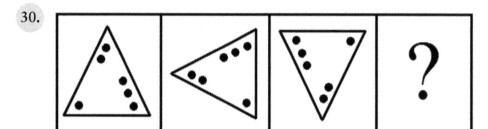

What is next?

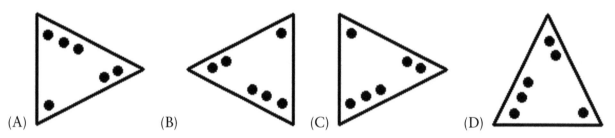

(A)   (B)   (C)   (D)

31. In the following series, find the number of common multiples of 4 and 6:

4, 8, 12, 20, 24, 28, 36, 42, 48, 54, 60.

(A) only three common multiples   (B) only four common multiples

(C) only five common multiples   (D) only six common multiples

32. How many balls are there?

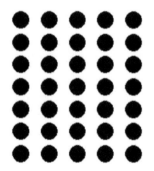

(A) 35 balls   (B) 25 balls   (C) 49 balls   (D) 50 balls

33. See this picture:

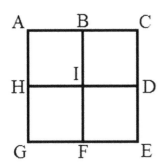

If the area of ABIH is 32 m², then what is the area of ACEG?

(A) 96 m² (B) 1,024 m² (C) 32 m² (D) 128 m²

34. Fill the <u>X</u> correctly:

```
    52
 ×  13
 ─────
   X X X
 X X X X
 ─────
   676
```

Find the option which is correct.

(A) $\begin{array}{r}156\\52\times\end{array}$ (B) $\begin{array}{r}26\\52\times\end{array}$ (C) $\begin{array}{r}65\\52\times\end{array}$ (D) $\begin{array}{r}156\\\times26\end{array}$

35. Simplify: $\dfrac{7}{100}$ = ?

(A) 7.00 (B) 0.7 (C) 0.007 (D) 0.07

36. According to the diagram, what is fraction of the colored area?

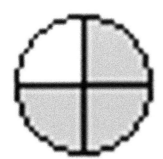

(A) $\dfrac{2}{3}$ (B) $\dfrac{1}{3}$ (C) $\dfrac{3}{4}$ (D) only 1

37. 937.56 – 234.09 = ?

(A) 700 (B) 306.99 (C) 802.91 (D) 703.47

38. If ∠SUT = 35°, then what is the value of ∠STU?

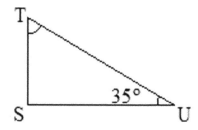

(A) ∠STU = 55°   (B) ∠STU = 45°   (C) ∠STU = 180°   (D) ∠STU = 90°

End of section.

If you have any time left, go over the questions in this section only.

Do not start the next section.

You have 25 minutes to answer the 25 questions in the Reading Comprehension and Vocabulary section.

Directions:

This section contains six short reading passages. Each passage is followed by six questions based on its content. Answer the questions following each passage on the basis of what is stated or implied in that passage. You may write in your test booklet.

Questions 1–6

Conservationists often have to educate the public about how to identify <u>invasive</u> species like the spotted lanternfly and Asian carp. But the Polish Academy of Sciences just added another animal to its list of invasive alien species, and it might be in the same room with you right now: the domestic cat.

To be designated an "invasive alien species," cats needed to meet two criteria: They had to be non-native, and they had to "cause economic or environmental harm or harm to human health." Cats actually meet both of these criteria, and not just in Poland. Here in the United States, too, felines can have a huge effect on the environment, and not in a good way.

This designation of the Polish Academy of Sciences is meant mostly for educational purposes and to inform policymaking. It in no way means that people in Poland can't have pet cats, but it is an important step in growing awareness about the significant ecological harm cats can cause.

The U.S. Department of Agriculture doesn't name cats in its partial listing of invasive species in the U.S., but it did say they are invasive in a paper published last year. These moves by the Polish Academy of Sciences and the USDA, while unwelcome by some cat lovers, are needed steps in addressing the problems caused by cats.

Scientific research shows that cats were likely domesticated in Middle Eastern farming villages, and from there people spread the species around the world. So the Polish Academy of Sciences considers them to be non-native—unlike the wildcat and lynx, which are both native to Poland.

So cats are "alien" in Poland, and the U.S. But cats are famous for helping people by eating pests like rats and mice (as well as being welcome companions to <u>frazzled</u> pet owners). Cats have even been used in American cities specifically for pest control. Some Chicago residents claim that a group of cats was the only thing that could keep their backyards rat-free.

1. The main objective of this passage is

   (A) to prove to readers that cats are invasive alien species in Poland and the U.S.

   (B) to advise people not to have cats as pets

   (C) to warn people that cats are harmful pets

   (D) to educate people that having cats as pets is banned

2. In line 2, what part of speech is the underlined word?

   (A) verb   (B) adjective   (C) noun   (D) adverb

3. In line 2, what does the underlined word mean?

   (A) occurring at irregular intervals or only in a few places; scattered or isolated

   (B) tending to spread especially in a quick or aggressive manner

   (C) occurring, appearing, or done infrequently and irregularly

   (D) occurring at irregular intervals; not continuous or steady

4. The passage gives enough information to answer which question?

   (A) What breeds of cats are considered aliens?   (B) When were cats banned as house pets?

   (C) Why are cats considered aliens?   (D) What dogs are aliens?

5. According to research, where were cats domesticated first?

   (A) Southeast Asia   (B) Japan   (C) Middle Eastern farming villages   (D) China

6. What does the underlined word in line 41 mean?

   (A) adjective   (B) adverb   (C) noun   (D) verb

Questions 7–12

In 2009, Congress took the important step of banning flavored cigarettes that <u>enticed</u> youth to start smoking. However, that landmark legislation contained a significant flaw: a loophole that allowed tobacco companies to continue selling menthol cigarettes.

For decades, tobacco companies have relied heavily on menthol flavoring—a chemical additive found in nature that can also be created in a laboratory—because menthol makes it easier to start smoking and harder to quit. When added to cigarettes, menthol produces a cooling effect that masks the harshness of cigarette smoke and allows the user to inhale more deeply at the same time that it can enhance the effects of nicotine, the addictive element in cigarettes.

The Food and Drug Administration is finally considering action to close this loophole for good, proposing rules earlier this year to end the sale of menthol cigarettes as well as all flavored cigars. The public comment period, during which the agency solicits feedback to inform potential implementation of the proposed rules, ends Tuesday. It is crucial that we speak out about ending menthol sales now—particularly because of the many Black lives that are at stake.

No doubt thanks to predatory marketing tactics over the past four generations—including billboards, point-of-sale promotions, corporate sponsorships, coupons and free samples concentrated in Black communities— approximately 85% of Black people who smoke use menthols.

The cigarette regulation loophole that disproportionately costs Black lives

The FDA is finally considering action. It's about time.

7. The main objective of this passage is

(A) to educate the readers of the action FDA has done to address the loophole on the flavored cigarette ban except for menthol

(B) to advise readers that menthol flavored cigarettes are less harmful than other flavored cigarettes

(C) to enumerate the flavors of cigarettes

(D) to inform readers that Black communities are top on the list of the greatest number of smokers

8. What year did the Congress ban flavored cigarettes?

(A) 2000s (B) 2009 (C) the 90s (D) unknown

9. What part of speech is the underlined word in line 2?

(A) noun (B) adjective (C) verb (D) adverb

10. What does the underlined word in line 2 mean?

(A) shoo (B) attracted (C) push (D) uninvite

11. What community is the menthol-flavored cigarette famous to?

(A) White (B) Hispanic (C) Asian (D) Black

12. Why is FDA proposing to ban all flavored cigarettes including menthol?

(A) because menthol produces a cooling effect that masks the harshness of cigarette smoke and allows the user to inhale more deeply at the same time that it can enhance the effects of nicotine, the addictive element in cigarettes

(B) because menthol is cheap and natural

(C) because menthol constitutes to the bigger portion of tobacco sales

(D) because menthol is less addictive

Questions 13–18

New evidence suggests our youngest working generation is going further than others to secure its economic future. A report just released by investment management company BlackRock reveals Generation Zers are already putting an average of 14% of their salary toward retirement. According to CNBC, this is a higher percentage than any other generation is saving right now.

This rate also exceeds what millennials did at the same age Gen Zers are now. 2021 research by Fidelity found that 15.8% of Gen Zers were investing in 401(k)s compared with 11.4% of millennials who did so at that life stage.

Gen Zers—the oldest of who are turning 25 this year—are <u>blazing</u> their own path when it comes to other aspects of career and work as well. Many are forgoing the traditional four-year college degree in favor of options like trade school and digital credentials. Compared with millennials and Gen Xers, recent research shows Gen Z is instead looking for "shorter, less expensive, more direct-to-career pathways in high-demand industries."

It's <u>noteworthy</u> but not surprising that America's youngest adults are charting a more pragmatic, thoughtful approach toward education, work and saving. After all, events that occur during our childhood, adolescence and early adulthood have a strong influence on our attitudes and behaviors—even stronger than things we experience later in life. For our oldest Gen Zers, that has meant growing up during a tide of dislocation—particularly of the economic variety.

13. The main objective of this passage is

(A) to cite that the Gen Zers have been more focused on securing their economic future compared to other generations at the same age

(B) to convince readers that the millennials are still the better generation

(C) to educate readers that putting off a degree in college is never a good idea

(D) to advise readers to learn from older generations

14. In line 15, what part of speech is the underlined word?

(A) noun   (B) verb   (C) adjective   (D) adverb

15. In line 15, what is the meaning of the underlined word?

(A) perform at moderate quality

(B) do something at an average speed

(C) achieve at an impressive manner   (D) casually perform a task

16. In line 24, what part of speech is the underlined word?

(A) noun (B) verb (C) preposition (D) adjective

17. In line 24, what is the meaning of the underlined word?

(A) interesting (B) boring (C) common (D) ordinary

18. The passage gives enough information to answer which question?

(A) How much do the Gen Zers put into retirement?

(B) What are the boomers doing these days?

(C) When does a Gen Z mature?

(D) Are the millennials more intelligent than the Gen Z?

Questions 19–25

When it comes to your child's backpack for school this year, experts are saying, "Lighten the load!"

Health experts told Fox News Digital that it is important parents be sure they're not sending their kids back to school with heavy, overweight book bags for this new school year, since heavy backpacks take more of a <u>toll</u> than many people may realize.

How much of a toll?

The U.S. Consumer Product Safety Commission says an estimated annual average of 7,500 kids under 19 years old were treated in emergency rooms for injuries related to backpacks from 2017 to 2019.

One parent of a 12-year-old girl told Fox News Digital that her daughter was <u>complaining</u> for months about upper back and neck pain.

At first, the Long Island, N.Y.-based mom thought her daughter's aches and pains were due to her sports activities.

But once they saw their physician, the mom learned her daughter's backpack was the <u>culprit</u>.

"She was picking up a backpack of books and going from classroom to classroom throughout the day and then carrying the bag to and from school. That's a lot of lifting," the mom told Fox News Digital.

Her daughter had to attend several weeks of sessions that included osteopathic manipulation to her spine for her neck and upper back strains.

She also had to start an exercise routine to strengthen her upper back to help support the load of the backpack.

19. The main objective of this passage is

   (A) to reprimand parents for making their children suffer

   (B) to educate parents to lighten children's backpacks as experts say

   (C) to warn parents that children will be lazy when given lighter load

   (D) to highlight that children need to carry backpacks

20. In line 8, what does the underlined word mean?

   (A) benefit (B) advantage (C) damage (D) use

21. In line 17, what part of speech is the underlined word?

   (A) noun (B) pronoun (C) adjective (D) verb

22. The passage gives enough information to answer which question?

   (A) How many kids were sent to the emergency rooms for backpack related injuries from 2017 to 2019?

   (B) What kind of backpack should a parent buy for their kid?

   (C) When should parents stop buying backpacks?

   (D) How heavy in kilograms should a backpack be?

23. In line 23, what does the underlined word mean?

   (A) innocent (B) offender (C) victim (D) casualty

24. What do experts advise when it comes to children's backpacks?

   (A) add more books (B) lighten the load (C) bring two bags for balance (D) no backpacks

25. How old were the children treated in the emergency rooms for backpack related injuries from 2017 to 2019?

   (A) under 19 years old (B) 19 years old and older (C) college students (D) 20–25 years old

End of section.

If you have any time left, go over the questions in this section only.

Do not start the next section.

You have 30 minutes to answer the 30 questions in the Mathematics Achievement Section.

Each question is followed by four suggested answers. Read each question and then decide which one of the four suggested answers is best.

Find the row of spaces on your document that has the same number as the question. In this row, mark the space having the same letter as the answer you have chosen. You may write in your test booklet.

SAMPLE QUESTION: Sample Answer

Which of the numbers below is not a factor of 364?   A ● C D

(A) 13
(B) 20
(C) 26
(D) 91

The correct answer is 20, so circle B is darkened.

---

1. Which function is equivalent to 11.60?

    (A) $\dfrac{116}{100}$ (B) $\dfrac{1,160}{1,000}$ (C) $11\dfrac{3}{5}$ (D) 12

2. What is the multiplication of 16.16 and 9.8?

    (A) 158.368   (B) 336.038   (C) 114.700   (D) 160.164

3. Which difference is between 120 and $\dfrac{7}{12}$?

    (A) $\dfrac{1,433}{24}$ (B) $\dfrac{1,400}{12}$ (C) 119.42   (D) 120

4. What is the value of the expression?

    (42 − 13 + 11 + 13 × 2) ÷ (34 ÷ 17)

    (A) 36   (B) 32   (C) 40   (D) 30

5. What is the standard form of eighty lakhs fifty-four thousand ninety-seven?

    (A) 8,054,098   (B) 8,045,089   (C) 8,454,898   (D) invalid number

6. Use the set of numbers shown to answer the question.

{34, 51, 68, 85, 102, ...}

Which describes this set of numbers?

(A) multiples of 17   (B) prime numbers   (C) even numbers   (D) odd numbers

7. The graph shows the number of hotdogs sold at a bakery bake sale.

Hours since Start of Sale	Hotdogs Sold
1	⊖ ⊖ ⊖ ⊖4
2	⊖ ⊖2
3	⊖ ⊖ ⊖ ⊖ ⊖ ⊖ ⊖7
4	⊖ ⊖ ⊖ ⊖ ⊖ ⊖ ⊖ ⊖ ⊖ ⊖ ⊖ ⊖12
5	⊖ ⊖ ⊖ ⊖ ⊖5

⊖ = 10 hotdogs sold

How many hotdogs were sold at the bake sale?

(A) 160   (B) 900   (C) 450   (D) 300

8. If (■ ÷ 17) × 37 = 2,331, what number does ■ stands for?

(A) 3,001   (B) –1,021   (C) 1,071   (D) ± 1,083

9. What is the name of a parallelogram whose sides are equal to each other but none of the angles are right angles?

(A) kite   (B) rhombus   (C) rectangle   (D) pentagon

10. In Mrs. William's class of 120 students, 36 students are allergic to bees. If a bee flies into the classroom and stings a student at random, what is the probability that the student is allergic to the bee?

(A) $\dfrac{3}{10}$ (B) $\dfrac{1}{10}$ (C) $\dfrac{1}{30}$ (D) 10

11. Which number is divisible by 15 without a remainder of 19?

(A) 214   (B) 238   (C) 244   (D) 274

12. If all sides of a triangle are equal and $\angle ACB = 60^\circ$, what is the summation of $\angle ABC$ and $\angle BAC$?

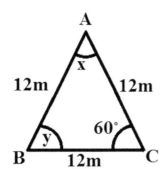

(A) 120° (B) 180° (C) 360° (D) 270°

13. If $\dfrac{1}{2^x} = 512$, then the value of $x = ?$

(A) 2^{-9} (B) $\dfrac{1}{3}$ (C) -3 (D) $\dfrac{1}{2^{-9}}$

14. Which of the following numbers is a multiple of 25?

(A) 225 (B) 155 (C) 305 (D) 630

15. Use the number line to answer the question.

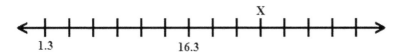

What number is represented by point "X" on the number line?

(A) 21.3 (B) 23.8 (C) 26.3 (D) 28.8

16. Which of the following is equal to $19 \times \dfrac{95}{361}$?

(A) $\dfrac{19 + 95}{19}$ (B) 5 (C) 19 (D) $\dfrac{361 \div 95}{19}$

17. Mr. Jack has 23.05 ft tall house. There are 12 in in 1 ft. How many inches tall is Mrs. Jack's house?

(A) 259. 35 (B) 651.02 (C) 166.09 (D) 276.60

18. James asked 1,000 students what their favorite footballers were. The chart below shows his result.

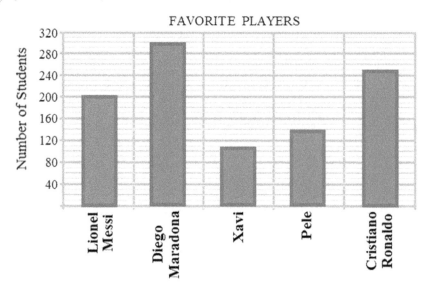

How many more students prefer Diego Maradona than Xavi and Pele combined?

(A) 50   (B) 20   (C) 30   (D) both are equal

19. What is the value of the expression: $(1,000 - 149 \times 3 + 247) \div 5$?

(A) 160   (B) 200   (C) 400   (D) 100

20. Miss. Alexey has 47 boxes of glitters. Each box contains 15 glitters. If X represents the total number of glitters, which equation would tell her how many glitters she has?

(A) $47 \times 15 = X$ (B) $X + 15 = 47$ (C) $50 = \dfrac{X}{17}$ (D) $X = \dfrac{15}{32}$

21. The chart below shows Sky's sales from the store in a week.

Item	Price per Item	Quantity
Party spray	$5.00	25 pieces
Birthday templates	$0.10	30 packets
Candles	$10.00	14 packets
Birthday ribbons	$12.02	6 boxes
Crayon	$52.00	4 boxes
Glitter	$50.20	5 boxes

What is the total cost?

(A) between $100 and $1,000   (B) above $16–$24 but below $1,060–$2,400

(C) between $2,400 and $3,200   (D) between $3,000 and $4,000

22. Lumi asked 1,200 first graders at her school where they want to go on the next school field trip. The table shows the results.

Field Trip Location	Number of Votes
Art museum	200
Public library	300
Animal shelter	210
Police station	240
Church	250

What fraction of the students wanted to go to either the art museum or the church?

(A) $\dfrac{1}{2}$ (B) $\dfrac{5}{25}$ (C) $\dfrac{16}{40}$ (D) $\dfrac{3}{8}$

23. What is the mode of this set of data?

TIME SPENT FOR READING IN WHOLE MONTH (IN HOURS)							
Week	Sunday	Monday	Tuesday	Wednesday	Thursday	Friday	Saturday
1	15	09	15	01	15	13	15
2	20	15	12	05	15	12	15
3	16	12	15	15	12	15	16
4	10	12	05	05	15	09	10

(A) 15 (B) 25 (C) 30 (D) 45

24. Shown below is a plan for a parking lot that a grocery store is building. Two angles shown in the plan are 60° and another two are 90°.

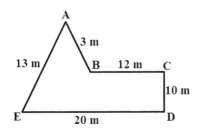

According to the grocery store's plan, what will be the perimeter (*P*) of the parking lot?

(A) 58 m (B) 32 m (C) 500 m (D) 60 m

25. Which of the following numbers is divisible by 13 without a remainder, but also by 7?

(A) 504 (B) 364 (C) 360 (D) 300

26. If the radius of a Circle is 2.5 meter. Then what is the area (A) of the circle, where $\pi = \dfrac{22}{7}$?

(A) 32.55 (B) 20.36 (C) 19.63 (D) None of above

27. Use the coordinate graph below

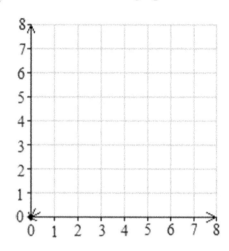

Alexa plotted the following points on the coordinate graph:
Point A (1, 2); Point B (1, 6); Point C (4, 6)
Where on the coordinate graph should he plot Point *D* so that her points from a rectangle with vertices *A, B, C,* and *D*, and the sides *AB, BC, CD,* and *DA*?

(A) 5, 6   (B) 4, 2   (C) 6, 5   (D) 5, 3

28. What is the value of the expression 9782.03 – 427.49?

(A) 5,409.03   (B) 9354.54   (C) 6,509.28   (D) 5,58.04

29. Use the number sequence to answer the question.

–7, –3, 1, __, 9, 13, 17, __.

(A) 4, 21   (B) 5. 35   (C) –5, 55   (D) 1, 11

30. Look at the series: 121, 144, 169, 196, _____, 256, 289, ... What will be the number to the fill the blanks

(A) 226   (B) 156   (C) 324   (D) 225

End of section.

If you have any time left, go over the questions in this section only.

Do not start the next section.

Essay Topic Sheet

The directions for the Essay portion of the ISEE are printed in the box below. Use the pre-lined pages on pages 91 and 92 for this part of the Practice Test.

You will have 30 minutes to plan and write an essay on the topic printed on the other side of this page. **Do not write on another topic. An essay on another topic is not acceptable.**

The essay is designed to give you an opportunity to show how well you can write. You should try to express your thoughts clearly. How well you write is much more important than how much you write, but you need to say enough for a reader to understand what you mean.

You will probably want to write more than a short paragraph. You should also be aware that a copy of your essay will be sent to each school that will be receiving your test results. You are to write only in the appropriate section of the answer sheet. Please write or print so that your writing may be read by someone who is not familiar with your handwriting.

You may make notes and plan your essay on the reverse side of the page. Allow enough time to copy the final form onto your answer sheet. You must copy the essay topic onto your answer sheet, in the box provided.

Please remember to write only the final draft of the essay on your answer sheet and to write it in blue or black pen. Again, you may use cursive writing, or you may print. Only pages 91 and 92 will be sent to the schools.

Directions continue on the next page.

REMINDER: Please write this essay topic on the first few lines of your answer sheet.

Essay Topic

Among the items you use or carry daily, which one is your most favorite item? Why did you choose this item?

- Only write on this essay question
- Only pages 91 and 92 will be sent to the schools
- Only write in blue or black pen

NOTES

_____
_____
_____
_____
_____
_____
_____
_____
_____
_____
_____
_____
_____
_____
_____
_____
_____
_____
_____
_____
_____
_____
_____

91

STUDENT NAME _____ GRADE APPLYING FOR _____

Use a blue or black ballpoint pen to write the final draft of your essay on this sheet.

You must write your essay topic in this space.

_____

_____

_____

Use specific details in your response

_____

_____

_____

_____

_____

_____

_____

_____

_____

_____

_____

_____

_____

_____

_____

_____

_____

_____

_____

_____

_____

_____

_____

_____

_____

_____

_____

_____

_____

End of section.

If you have any time left, go over the questions in this section only.

ANSWER KEY

Verbal Reasoning

1. B	7. A	13. D	19. C	25. B	31. C
2. C	8. A	14. A	20. C	26. C	32. A
3. A	9. C	15. C	21. B	27. A	33. B
4. D	10. D	16. C	22. A	28. B	34. B
5. D	11. B	17. B	23. D	29. D	
6. B	12. B	18. A	24. A	30. A	

1. The correct answer is (B). Acceptable means adequate; satisfactory. Sample: "an acceptable substitute for champagne"

2. The correct answer is (C). To accompany someone means to go somewhere with (someone) as a companion or escort. Sample: "The two sisters were to accompany us to New York."

3. The correct answer is (A). An advantage is a favorable or desirable circumstance or feature, a benefit.

4. The correct answer is (D). Amusing means causing laughter and providing entertainment.

5. The correct answer is (D). Ancient means having been in existence for a very long time.

6. The correct answer is (B). To animate is to bring to life. It also means to give inspiration, encouragement, or renewed vigor to. Sample: "She has animated the nation with a sense of political direction."

7. The correct answer is (A). To be anxious is to experience worry, unease, or nervousness, typically about an imminent event or something with an uncertain outcome.

8. The correct answer is (A). To argue is to exchange or express diverging or opposite views, typically in a heated or angry way.

9. The correct answer is (C). To arrest is commonly used as to seize (someone) by legal authority and take into custody. It also means to stop or check (progress or a process).

10. The correct answer is (D). To be ashamed means to be reluctant to do something through fear of embarrassment or humiliation.

11. The correct answer is (B). To attempt means to make an effort to achieve or complete (something, typically a difficult task or action).

12. The correct answer is (B). The direct meaning of baggage is personal belongings packed in suitcases for traveling, luggage. It also means past experiences or long-held ideas regarded as burdens and impediments.

13. The correct answer is (D). Basic means something forming an essential foundation or starting point; fundamental. Sample: "Certain basic rules must be obeyed."

14. The correct answer is (A). To behave is to conduct oneself in accordance with the accepted norms of a society or group. Sample: "they were expected to behave themselves"

15. The correct answer is (C). To believe is to accept (something) as true; feel sure of the truth of.

16. The correct answer is (C). To bet is to risk something, usually a sum of money, against someone else's based on the outcome of a future event, such as the result of a race or game. It means to feel sure. Sample: "I bet this place is really spooky late at night."

17. The correct answer is (B). To block is to make the movement or flow in (a passage, pipe, road, etc.) difficult or impossible. Sample: "block up the holes with sticky tape"

18. The correct answer is (A). To get over means to recover from an ailment or an upsetting or startling experience. In this sentence, drinking was the subject's way to try to recover from the canceled engagement.

19. The correct answer is (C). To get up means to rise from bed after sleeping.

20. The correct answer is (C). To turn down means to reject something offered or proposed.

21. The correct answer is (B). To turn up means to put in an appearance; arrive.

22. The correct answer is (A). To turn back means to go back in the direction from which one has come.

23. The correct answer is (D). To run over means to knock a person or animal down and pass over their body. Sample: "I almost ran over that raccoon."

24. The correct answer is (A). The preposition "for" is used to indicate the use of something, to mean because of, to indicate time or duration. In this sentence, the speaker was waiting because of someone he knows.

25. The correct answer is (B). The preposition "to" is used to indicate the place, person, or thing that someone or something moves toward, or the direction of something, to indicate a limit or an ending point, to indicate relationship, and to indicate a time or a period. In this sentence, someone is asked to go to a direction which is the bed.

26. The correct answer is (C). A bin is a receptacle in which to deposit trash or recyclables.

27. The correct answer is (A). Lien refers to an official order that allows someone to keep the property of a person who owes them money until it has been paid. Sample: "The bank intends to hold a lien on the entire balance for the $400 due."

28. The correct answer is (B). Lean, if used as an adjective, means (of a person or animal) thin, especially healthily so, having no superfluous fat or (of meat) containing little fat. Sample: "lean bacon"

29. The correct answer is (D). To be commended means to be praised formally or officially.

30. The correct answer is (A). To commit means to carry out or perpetrate (a mistake, crime, or immoral act).

31. The correct answer is (C). To comment is to express (an opinion or reaction).

32. The correct answer is (A). Calm down is a common phrasal verb which means to relax after an energetic or irritated state.

33. The correct answer is (B). To come around means to change an opinion or see a new point of view.

34. The correct answer is (B). To come up with means to think of an idea, especially as the first person to do so, or to produce a solution.

Quantitative Reasoning

1. D	11. C	21. A	31. C
2. B	12. A	22. B	32. A
3. D	13. A	23. C	33. D
4. D	14. B	24. B	34. A
5. B	15. D	25. C	35. D
6. A	16. B	26. B	36. C
7. C	17. D	27. D	37. D
8. D	18. A	28. B	38. A
9. A	19. C	29. C	
10. A	20. C	30. C	

1. The correct answer is (D). This is an alternating number of subtraction series. First, 1 is subtracted then 2 is added.

   The pattern is: 12 − 1 = 11; 11 + 2 = 13; 13 − 1 = 12; 12 + 2 = 14; 14 − 1 = 13; 13 + 2 = 15 …

2. The correct answer is (B). In this question, it's clearly mentioned that Poppy chooses six different colored socks. Out of them she chooses nine white socks, and the rest are different five color socks. So, 9 white socks and 45 other socks is true.

3. The correct answer is (D). We know, half of the area of square = $\dfrac{4 \times length}{2}$ unit.

   So, $\dfrac{4 \times 29}{2}$ cm is true.

4. The correct answer is (D).

   L.C.M. of all denominators is 240

   So, $2\dfrac{1}{2} = \dfrac{5 \times 120}{2 \times 120} = \dfrac{600}{240} = 600$

   $\dfrac{1.3}{8} = \dfrac{13}{8 \times 10} = \dfrac{13 \times 3}{80 \times 3}$

   $1\dfrac{2}{3} = \dfrac{5 \times 80}{3 \times 80} = \dfrac{400}{240}$

   $\dfrac{1}{10} = \dfrac{1 \times 24}{10 \times 24} = \dfrac{24}{240}$

   So, the lowest fraction is $\dfrac{1}{10}$.

5. The correct answer is (B). $154 \div 14 − 7 \times 3 + 25 = 11 − 7 \times 3 + 25 = 11 − 21 + 25 = (11 + 25) − 21 = 36 − 21 = 15$.

6. The correct answer is (A).

   We know, $56 \div 14 = 4$; or $4 \times 14 = 56$, $x \times 14 = 4 \times 14$, or $x = 4$

   Similarly,

   $126 \div 14 = 9$; or $9 \times 14 = 126$, $x \times 14 = 9 \times 14$, or $x = 9$.

7. The correct answer is (C). $(12 \div 6) + 3 \times 7 = 42 \Rightarrow (12 + 6) \div 3 \times 7 = 18 \div 3 \times 7 = 6 \times 7 = 42$.

8. The correct answer is (D).

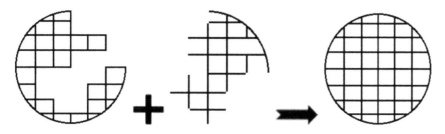

9. The correct answer is (A).

$$2x - 5 = 45; \Rightarrow x = \frac{45 - 5}{2} = 20;$$

$$3y + 13 = 112; \Rightarrow y = \frac{112 - 13}{3} = 33;$$

$$\Rightarrow 3x + 2y = (3 \times 20) - (2 \times 33) = 159.$$

10. The correct answer is (A).

$15\,L \Rightarrow 150\,km$

$\Rightarrow 1\,L \Rightarrow (150/15)\,km = 10\,km$

$\Rightarrow 10\,L \Rightarrow (10 \times 10)\,km = 100\,km.$

11. The correct answer is (C). $(2 \times 3) + 4 = 10$, and so on. So $(\varnothing \times 3) + 4 = \oplus$ is correct.

12. The correct answer is (A). Total area is 96 m², the area of each small triangle 96 ÷ 16 = 6 m². Now there are six shaded small squares; so, the area of those shaded triangle = 6 × 6 m² = 36 m².

13. The correct answer is (A). $605 \div \frac{15}{36} \times 12 = \frac{605 \times 36 \times 12}{15}$.

14. The correct answer is (B). $A = (5 + 5) = 10$; $B = (10 + 5) = 15$; $C = (20 + 10 + 5) = 35$
Now, $(10 + 15 + 35) \div 3 = 20$.

15. The correct answer is (D).

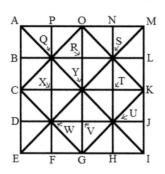

Number of squares are: ABQP, PQRO, ORNS, NSLM, BCXQ, QXYR, RYTS, STKL, CDWX, XWVY, YVUT, TUJK, DEFW, WFGV, VGUH, UHIJ, ACYO, OYKM, CEGY, YGIK, QWUS.

Thus, there are 21 squares.

16. The correct answer is (B). $18 : 12 :: 36 : x \Rightarrow 8/12 = 36/x \Rightarrow x = \dfrac{36 \times 12}{18} = 24$.

17. The correct answer is (D). $\sqrt{y} + \sqrt{64} = 9.39 \Rightarrow \pi = 9.39 - 8; \Rightarrow y = 1.93$ (approx.).

18. The correct answer is (A). $(11 + 3 + 9 + 35 + 16 + 20) \div 6 = 15.67$ (approx.).

19. The correct answer is (C). Number of students in the class = 80

    Oscar's rank from the last $\Rightarrow$50th

    Mia's rank ahead of Alex $\Rightarrow$2th

    or, Mia's rank from the last $\Rightarrow$(50 + 2) = 52th

    $\Rightarrow$ia's rank from the beginning 80 – 52 + 1 = 37th.

20. The correct answer is (C). $\sqrt[4]{625} \div 5 - 2 + 14 = 25 \div 5 - 2 + 14 = 5 - 2 + 14 = 17$.

21. The correct answer is (A). $25*2*6 = 4*11*0 \Leftrightarrow 25 \times 2 - 6 = 4 \times 11 + 0$.

    L.H.S. $\Rightarrow 25 \times 2 - 6 = 50 - 6 = \underline{44} \Leftrightarrow$ R.H.S. $\Rightarrow 4 \times 11 + 0 = 44 + 0 = \underline{44}$.

22. The correct answer is (B). $10 - 3 + 5 = 12$; $12 - 4 + 5 = 13$; $14 - 5 + 5 = 14$; then $16 - 6 + 5 = 15$.

23. The correct answer is (C).

    $[\{12 + (7 \times 4)\} \div 4 + \{(6 \times 9) \div 3\}] \div 4$

    $= [\{12 + 28\} \div 4 + \{54 \div 3\}] \div 4$

    $= [40 \div 4 + 18] \div 4$

    $= [10 + 18] \div 4$

    $= 28 \div 4 = 7$ (Answer).

24. The correct answer is (B). (31 + 64 + 21 + 9 + 12 + 3) ÷ 6 = 23.33 (approx.).

25. The correct answer is (C).

    10 = 2 × 5

    25 = 5 × 5

    So, the greatest common factor of 10, 25 is 5.

26. The correct answer is (B). $60 \times A\% = 15 \Rightarrow A = \dfrac{15}{60} \times 100 = 25$.

27. The correct answer is (D). 62.92 × 0.0736 = 4.630912.

28. The correct answer is (B).

    $2 \Rightarrow 2 + 2 + 1 = 5$

    $5 \Rightarrow 5 + 2 + 1 = 8$

    $8 \Rightarrow + 2 + 1 = 11$

    $11 \Rightarrow 11 + 2 + 1 = \underline{14}$.

29. The correct answer is (C).

    If Andrew takes 15 days to finish his work

    Andrew's one day work = 1/15

    Similarly, Bruno's one day work = 1/10

    Now, total work done by Andrew and Bruno in a day = 1/15 + 1/10

    Taking L.C.M. (15, 10), we have:

    A day's work of Andrew and Bruno = $(2 + 3)/30 = \dfrac{1}{6}$

    $\Rightarrow$ Andrew and Bruno can finish the work in six days if they work together.

30. The correct answer is (C). The triangle rotates anticlockwise. So, Option "C" is true.

31. The correct answer is (C). 4, 8, <u>12</u>, 20, <u>24</u>, 28, <u>36</u>, 42, <u>48</u>, 54, and <u>60</u>: in this series, only the underlined numbers are divisible by 4 and 6 both.

32. The correct answer is (A).

```
   52
 × 13
 ───
  156
  52×
 ───
  676
```

5 × 7 = 35 balls are there.

33. The correct answer is (D). As, ABIH = BCDI = DEFI = FGHI.

So, ACEG = (32 m² × 4) = 128 m²

34. The correct answer is (A).

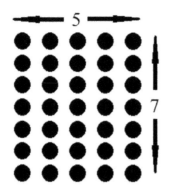

35. The correct answer is (D). $\frac{7}{100}$ =

```
100 | 700 | 0.07
    | 700 |
    | ─── |
    |  ×  |
```

36. The correct answer is (C). As per the diagram, the circle has four parts and among them three are colored. So, the fraction will be $\frac{3}{4}$.

37. The correct answer is (D). 937.56 – 234.09 = 703.47.

38. The correct answer is (A).

We know the total of all angles of a triangle is 180°.

Here, ∠SUT = 35° and ∠TSU = 90°

So, ∠STU = 180° – (∠SUT + ∠TSU) = 180° – (35° + 90°) = 55°.

Reading Comprehension and Vocabulary

1. A	6. A	11. D	16. D	21. D
2. B	7. A	12. A	17. A	22. A
3. B	8. B	13. A	18. A	23. B
4. C	9. C	14. B	19. B	24. B
5. D	10. B	15. C	20. C	25. A

1. The correct answer is (A). The passage is from a news article regarding cats being an invasive alien species. See lines 3–15.

2. The correct answer is (B). Invasive is an adjective which means (especially of plants or a disease) tending to spread prolifically and undesirably or harmfully.

3. The correct answer is (B). Invasive is an adjective which means (especially of plants or a disease) tending to spread prolifically and undesirably or harmfully.

4. The correct answer is (C). See line 38. "So cats are 'alien' in Poland, and the U.S."

5. The correct answer is (D). See lines 31–32.

6. The correct answer is (A). Frazzled is an adjective which means showing the effects of exhaustion or strain. Sample: "a long line of screaming children and frazzled parents"

7. The correct answer is (A). See lines 18–22. The passage educates us on how the FDA has finally taken an action to propose banning of all flavored cigarettes including menthol which is most popular among the Black communities and equally care for all communities.

8. The correct answer is (B). See line 1.

9. The correct answer is (C). To entice is a verb which means to attract or tempt by offering pleasure or advantage. "Enticed" is its past tense.

10. The correct answer is (B). To entice is to attract or tempt by offering pleasure or advantage.

11. The correct answer is (D). See lines 33–35.

12. The correct answer is (A). See lines 11–17.

13. The correct answer is (A). The passage is highlighting how the Gen Zers are securing their economic future compared to millennials and Gen X at the same age.

14. The correct answer is (B). Blazing is used as a verb in the line which means achieve something in an impressive manner.

15. The correct answer is (C). Blazing is used as a verb in the line which means achieve something in an impressive manner.

16. The correct answer is (D). Noteworthy is an adjective which means interesting, significant, or unusual.

17. The correct answer is (A). Noteworthy is an adjective which means interesting, significant, or unusual.

18. The correct answer is (A). See lines 5–6.

19. The correct answer is (B). See lines 1–3.

20. The correct answer is (C). A toll refers to the cost or damage resulting from something. Sample: "The environmental toll of the policy has been high."

21. The correct answer is (D). To complain is to express dissatisfaction or annoyance about something. Complaining in the line is used as the action word of the subject "daughter."

22. The correct answer is (A). See lines 11–15.

23. The correct answer is (B). Culprit means a person who is responsible for a crime or other misdeed or the cause of a problem or defect. Sample: "Viruses could turn out to be the culprit."

24. The correct answer is (B). See lines 1–3.

25. The correct answer is (A). See lines 11–15.

Mathematics Achievement

1. C	11. B	21. D
2. A	12. A	22. D
3. C	13. D	23. A
4. B	14. A	24. A
5. A	15. B	25. B
6. A	16. B	26. C
7. D	17. D	27. B
8. C	18. A	28. B
9. B	19. A	29. A
10. A	20. A	30. D

1. The correct answer is (C). $11.60 = \dfrac{1,160}{100} \Leftrightarrow 1,160 \div 100 = 11\dfrac{3}{5}$.

2. The correct answer is (A). $16.16 \times 9.8 = 158.368$.

3. The correct answer is (C). The difference between 120 and $\dfrac{7}{12}$ is $= \dfrac{1,440 - 7}{12} = \dfrac{1,433}{12} = 119.42$ (approx.).

4. The correct answer is (B). $(42 - 13 + 11 + 13 \times 2) \div (34 \div 17) = (42 - \cancel{13} + 11 + \cancel{13} \times 2) \div (34 \div 17) = (42 + 11 \times 2) \div (34 \div 17) = (42 + 22) \div 2 = 64 \div 2 = 32$.

5. The correct answer is (A). The standard form of eighty lakhs fifty-four thousand ninety-seven is 8,054,098.

6. The correct answer is (A). The set of the multiples of 17 are 17, 34, 51, 68, 85, 102, and so on.

7. The correct answer is (D). The total number of pies sold $= 30 \times 10 = 300$.

8. The correct answer is (C). $(\blacksquare \div 17) \times 37 = 2,331$; Let $x = \blacksquare$;

   $\dfrac{x}{17} \times 37 = 2,331$; $x = \dfrac{(2,331 \times 17)}{37}$; $\Rightarrow x = 63 \times 17 = 1,071$.

9. The correct answer is (B). We know that a rhombus is a parallelogram whose sides are equal to each other but none of the angles are right angles.

10. The correct answer is (A). Thirty-six students are allergic to bees; there are 120 students, then the probability of bee stinging an allergic student is $= \dfrac{36}{120} = \dfrac{3}{10}$.

11. The correct answer is (B). Only if we divide 238 by 15, the remainder will be 13 not 19.

12. The correct answer is (A). We know the equilateral triangle has equal sides and equal angles. And the summation of all angles is 180°.

    So, if $\angle ACB = 60°$, then as per the rule $\angle ACB$ and $\angle ACB$ have the same value 60°.

    $\angle ACB + \angle ACB = 60° + 60° = 120°$.

13. The correct answer is (D). $\frac{1}{2^x} = 512 \Rightarrow \frac{1}{2^x} = 2^9 \Rightarrow 2^x = \frac{1}{2^{-9}} \Rightarrow \Rightarrow = \frac{1}{2^{-9}}$.

14. The correct answer is (A). The multiple of 25 is 225.

15. The correct answer is (B). $(1.3 + 2.5) = 3.8$, $(3.8 + 2.5) = 6.3$, $(6.3 + 2.5) = 8.8$, $(8.8 + 2.5) = 11.3$, $(11.3 + 2.5) = 13.8$, $(13.8 + 2.5) = 16.3$, $(16.3 + 2.5) = 18.8$, $(18.8 + 2.5) = 21.3$, $(21.3 + 2.5) = 23.8$, and so on. . 23.8 is the right answer.

16. The correct answer is (B). $19 \times \frac{95}{361} = \frac{19 \times 95}{361} = 5$.

17. The correct answer is (D). 1 ft = 12 in; $(23.05 \times 12 \text{ in}) = 276.60$ in.

18. The correct answer is (A). The total number of students like Diego Maradona = 300, Xavi = 110, and Pele = 140. So $\{300 - (110 + 140)\} = 50$ more students like Diego Maradona than Xavi and Pele combined.

19. The correct answer is (A). $(1,000 - 149 \times 3 + 247) \div 5 = 160$.

20. The correct answer is (A). There are 47 boxes; each box has 15 glitters. $X = (47 \times 15)$.

21. The correct answer is (D). $(\$5.00 \times 25) + (\$0.10 \times 30) + (\$10.00 \times 14) + (\$12.02 \times 6) + (\$52.00 \times 4) + (\$50.20 \times 5) = \$3,237.00$.

22. The correct answer is (D). The total number of students who wanted to go to art museum or church is = $200 + 250 = 450$. Total number of students = 1,200. Then the ratio is $\frac{15}{40} = \frac{3}{8}$.

23. The correct answer is (A). Fifteen occurs maximum time, so the mode is 15.

24. The correct answer is (A). Perimeter = Addition of all sides. $P = \{3 + 12 + 10 + 20 + 13\}$ m = 58 m.

25. The correct answer is (B). Among the options only 364 is divisible by 13 and 7 both. So, it is the answer.

26. The correct answer is (C). We know the area of a circle is πr^2.

Here $\pi = \dfrac{22}{7}$,

Therefore, A $= \pi r^2 = \dfrac{22}{7} \times 2.5^2 = 19.63495 = 19.63$ (approx.).

27. The correct answer is (B).

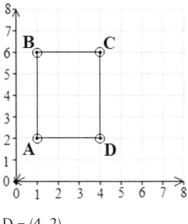

D = (4, 2).

28. The correct answer is (B). 9,782.03 – 427.49 = 9,354.54.

29. The correct answer is (A). Here we can see that the difference between each term is 4. Hence 4 and 21 will be the missing numbers.

30. The correct answer is (D). The pattern in this series is made by the square of the numbers 11, 12, 13, 14, 15, 16, 17, ..., n. Then the missing number will be $15^2 = 225$.

Sample Essay Response

Among the items I use daily, my most favorite is my phone. It might be the most cliché answer, but I have many reasons. I have owned this phone for more than 5 years and it reminds me how long me and my husband have been together.

I got my phone a few months after we became a couple. It was the first brand new phone I purchased using my heard earned money. Up to this date, it still works amazing, and I owe it to myself for taking good care of it.

There are several answers why a phone can be someone's favorite. Modern phones can now do more than sending SMS and calling someone. At the height of the pandemic, everybody stayed at home and our phones became our little helpers.

With just a few taps you can pay your bills, manage your finances, purchase an item and do your groceries. Phones became a staple item. You can transact for business or attend classes on your phone. Nowadays, phones are less used for leisure. Technology has given us countless advantages but just like any good thing, it gets bad when abused or used the wrong way. There are many studies proving how technology, or phones, can be detrimental to one's well-being and relationships with significant others. I believe that technology can be both beneficial and hazardous but it's up to you, which outcome you would bring yourself to. Will you bring yourself harm or will you reap its advantages?

For the ISEE, the most commonly referenced score is the stanine score. Check out the four steps to calculating stanine scores.

Step 1: The Raw Score

The first step in scoring is calculating a raw score. This is quite simple.

Students receive one point for each correct answer and no points for incorrect answers or unanswered questions.

Tip: Because there is no score penalty for incorrect answers or unanswered questions, be sure to answer every single question! Answering all of the questions can only increase your chances of a higher score.

Step 2: The Scaled Score

Once a raw score has been calculated for each section, it is converted into a scaled score.

This conversion adjusts for the variation in difficulty between different tests. Thus, a lower raw score on a harder test could give you the same scaled score as a higher raw score on an easier test. This process is called equating.

The scaled score for each section ranges from 760 to 940.

Step 3: The Percentile Score

Next, the percentile score for each section is calculated.

Percentiles compare a student's scaled score to all other same-grade students from the past three years. This is important to understand because the ISEE is taken by students in a range of grades. The Upper Level ISEE, for instance, is taken by students applying to grades 9–12; however, the percentile score is based only on the performance of other students applying to the same grade. Thus, a student applying to 9th grade will not be compared to a student applying to 12th grade.

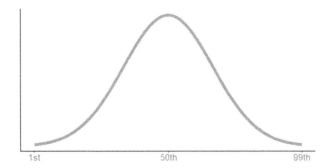

Here's an example to help understand percentile scores: scoring in the 40th percentile indicates that a student scored the same or higher than 40% of students in the same grade but lower than 59% of students.

Step 4: The Stanine Score

Finally, the percentile is converted into a stanine score.

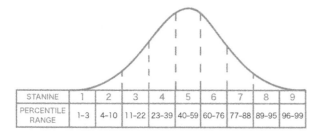

Notice that the percentile ranges for the middle stanines of 4–6 are far larger than the ranges for the extreme stanines of 1, 2, 8, or 9. This means that most students taking the ISEE achieve scores in the middle ranges. Only the top 4% of all test takers receive a stanine of 9 on any given section, while 20% of students receive a stanine of 5.

So, what is a good ISEE score?

Stanine scores (which range from 1 to 9) are the most important and are the scores schools pay the most attention to. But what is a good score on the ISEE? A score of 5 or higher will be enough to put students in the running for most schools, although some elite private schools want applicants to have ISEE test results of 7 or higher.

Here's a sample ISEE Report

Individual Student Report

Candidate for Grade	8
ID Number	
Gender	Male
Date of Birth	4/8/2004
Phone Number	
Test Level/Form	Middle/0916
Date of Testing	11/30/2016
Tracking Number	201612010592103

The Test Profile below shows your total scores for each test. Refer to the enclosed brochure called *Understanding the Individual Student Report* to help you interpret the *Test Profile* and *Analysis*. Percentile Ranks and Stanines are derived from norms for applicants to independent schools.

TEST PROFILE

Section	Scaled Score (760 – 940)	Percentile Rank (1 – 99)	Stanine (1 – 9)	Stanine Analysis 1 2 3 4 5 6 7 8 9
Verbal Reasoning	895	90	8	▬▬V▬
Reading Comprehension	890	76	6	▬R▬
Quantitative Reasoning	894	81	7	▬Q▬
Mathematics Achievement	883	61	6	▬M▬

LEGEND: V = Verbal Reasoning   R = Reading Comprehension   Q = Quantitative Reasoning   M = Mathematics Achievement

ANALYSIS

Section & Subsection	# of Questions	# Correct	Results for Each Question
Verbal Reasoning			
Synonyms	18	15	+++++++- ++++- ++- +
Single Word Response	17	16	++++++++++++- +++++
Quantitative Reasoning			
Word Problems	18	11	+++- - - +++- +++++- - -
Quantitative Comparisons	14	14	++++++++++++++
Reading Comprehension			
Main Idea	4	4	++++
Supporting Ideas	6	5	- +++++
Inference	6	5	+- ++++
Vocabulary	7	5	+++- +- +
Organization/Logic	4	4	++++
Tone/Style/Figurative Language	3	3	+++
Mathematics Achievement			
Whole Numbers	7	4	+- +++- -
Decimals, Percents, Fractions	9	5	++- - ++- - +
Algebraic Concepts	11	7	+++++- ++- - -
Geometry	4	2	+- +-
Measurement	5	4	++++-
Data Analysis and Probability	6	4	+++- +-

LEGEND: + = Correct   - = Incorrect   S = Skipped   N = Not Reached

The test was administered in the order reported in the analysis section; Verbal Reasoning, Quantitative Reasoning, Reading Comprehension, and Mathematics Achievement. Each section was divided into subsections, grouping similar types of questions. The Reading Comprehension subsection grouping does not represent the actual order of the test questions.

The above is a preliminary ISEE report. ERB reserves the right to amend this report before it is finalized. The report will be final no later than 20 business days. The final report will automatically be generated electronically.

ISEE—Lower Level Exam-3

Verbal Reasoning

You have 20 minutes to answer the 34 questions in the Verbal Reasoning Section.

This section is divided into two parts that contain two different types of questions. As soon as you have completed Part I, answer the questions in Part II. You may write in your test booklet. For each answer you select, fill in the corresponding circle on your answer document.

Part I—Synonyms

Each question in Part I consists of a word in capital letters followed by four answer choices. Select the one word that is most nearly the same in meaning as the word in capital letters.

SAMPLE QUESTION: <u>Sample Answer</u>

CHARGE: A   B   ●   D

(A) release
(B) belittle
(C) accuse
(D) conspire

Part II—Sentence Completion

Each question in Part II is made up of a sentence with one blank. Each blank indicates that a word or phrase is missing. The sentence is followed by four answer choices. Select the word or phrase that will best complete the meaning of the sentence as a whole.

SAMPLE QUESTIONS: <u>Sample Answer</u>

It rained so much that the streets were _____.   ●   B   C   D

(A) flooded
(B) arid
(C) paved
(D) crowded

The house was so dirty that it took _____.   A   B   C   ●

(A) less than 10 min to wash it
(B) four months to demolish it
(C) over a week to walk across it
(D) two days to clean it

Part I—Synonyms

Directions:

Select the word that is most nearly the same in meaning as the word in capital letters.

1. CIVIC

   (A) public (B) private (C) institutionalized (D) restricted

2. COINCIDENCE

   (A) planned (B) chance (C) organized (D) unlikelihood

3. COMMEND

   (A) criticize (B) bash (C) compliment (D) condemn

4. COMPACT

   (A) loose (B) movable (C) detached (D) firm

5. CONSENT

   (A) disallow (B) forbid (C) prohibit (D) allow

6. CONSPICUOUS

   (A) hidden (B) tiny (C) visible (D) unnoticed

7. DELUGE

   (A) limit (B) overwhelm (C) prohibit (D) scarce

8. DEPLETE

   (A) expend (B) augment (C) increase (D) add

9. DENSE

   (A) thin (B) light (C) concentrated (D) diluted

10. DEVISE

(A) break   (B) destroy   (C) design   (D) equipment

11. DETERIORATE

(A) improve   (B) degenerate   (C) progress   (D) develop

12. DIMINISH

(A) increase   (B) decline   (C) flare up   (D) boost

13. DISMANTLE

(A) build   (B) assemble   (C) gather   (D) deconstruct

14. DISSOLVE

(A) appear   (B) stick   (C) emerge   (D) vanish

15. DRAWBACK

(A) disadvantage   (B) advantage   (C) benefit   (D) edge

16. DRASTIC

(A) extreme   (B) slight   (C) little   (D) mild

17. EDIBLE

(A) poisonous   (B) toxic   (C) consumable   (D) rotten

Part II—Sentence Completion

Directions:

Select the word that best completes the sentence.

18. The radio station _____ to announce the winner of the million-dollar lottery.

(A) broke in   (B) broke off   (C) broke up   (D) broke into

19. The bride is about to _____ the wedding after finding out the groom doesn't want to move out of his parents' house.

(A) call up   (B) call on   (C) call off   (D) check in

20. I expect you to _____ when you volunteered to come with me to the community outreach program.

(A) check in   (B) check out   (C) call up   (D) chip in

21. Mom is _____ you to watch over the house while we're on vacation.

(A) cheering up   (B) counting on   (C) crossing out   (D) cutting back

22. The doctor recommended to _____ on unhealthy fats and choose lean meat.

(A) cut back   (B) cross out   (C) cut in   (D) check out

23. The students had to _____ their project as their classroom got flooded.

(A) do over   (B) cross over   (C) come over   (D) bring up

24. It's time to _____ with these outgrown clothes or donate them.

(A) do over   (B) do away   (C) dress up   (D) drop off

25. She quickly _____ and put on her fine jewelry to join her husband to a fancy dinner.

(A) dropped back   (B) dropped by   (C) dressed up   (D) dropped out

26. Dad bought a new pair of shoes to replace the one I _____.

(A) grew out of   (B) grew up with   (C) grew into   (D) grew back

27. Do not use your _____ hands when handling chemicals.

(A) bear (B) bare (C) bar (D) beer

28. The eldest daughters seem to _____ the responsibility of being the second mother of the family.

(A) bear (B) bare (C) bare (D) beer

29. It was his wife who _____ him to create a union against their cruel employer.

(A) cited (B) sighted (C) incited (D) insighted

30. The meeting's goal is to get _____ into the employees' behavior.

(A) cite (B) sight (C) incite (D) insight

31. She discovered the ring is not _____.

(A) real (B) reel (C) rail (D) rile

32. They needed a _____ of film for the shoot today.

(A) real (B) reel (C) rail (D) rile

33. The dog circled around chasing its _____ .

(A) till (B) tile (C) tail (D) tale

34. Grandpa told us _____ of his travels when he was young.

(A) tills (B) tiles (C) tails (D) tales

End of section.

If you have any time left, go over the questions in this section only.

Do not start the next section.

You have 35 minutes to answer the 38 questions in the Quantitative Reasoning Section.

Each question is followed by four suggested answers. Read each question and then decide which one of the four suggested answers is best.

Find the row of spaces on your document that has the same number as the question. In this row, mark the space having the same letter as the answer you have chosen. You may write in your test booklet.

EXAMPLE 1:   Sample Answer

What is the value of the expression (4 + 6) ÷ 2?   A   B   ●   D

(A) 2
(B) 4
(C) 5
(D) 7

The correct answer is 5, so circle C is darkened.

EXAMPLE 2:

A square has an area of 25 cm². What is the length of one of its side?   A   ●   C   D

(A) 1 cm
(B) 5 cm
(C) 10 cm
(D) 25 cm

The correct answer is 5 cm, so circle B is darkened.

---

1. See this picture:

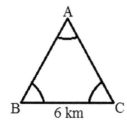

If AB is 6 km and all the angles are 60°. Then what is the perimeter of the triangle?

(A) 6 km   (B) 10 km   (C) 9 km   (D) 18 km

2. If A means "–," B means "+," C means "×," and D means "÷," then what is the value of [{(222 D 11) B 19} C 9] A 31?

(A) 335   (B) 158   (C) 242   (D) 157

3. Assemble given series in ascending order:
20, 38, 9, 16, 38
Find the option which is correct.

(A) 9, 16, 20, 36, 38   (B) 16, 9, 36, 38, 20   (C) 38, 36, 20, 16, 9   (D) none of the above

4. Simplify: $\left(\dfrac{1}{7}+\dfrac{5}{7}\right)-\left(\dfrac{1}{5}+\dfrac{2}{5}\right)$.

(A) $\dfrac{14}{35}$ (B) $\dfrac{28}{81}$ (C) $\dfrac{7}{35}$ (D) $\dfrac{9}{34}$

5. Simplify:
24 ÷ 4 (6 – 3) – 24 ÷ 4 (6 – 3)

(A) 16   (B) 0   (C) 14   (D) none of the above

6. The greatest common factor of 11, 55, and 121 is

(A) 10 and 11   (B) 2 and 5   (C) 1 and 11   (D) 1 and 12

7. What is the G.C.D. of 13, 65, 78, and 104?

(A) 20   (B) 26   (C) 30   (D) 13

8. Some equations are solved according to the specific method. Solve the unsolved equation following this method: If 20 – 9 + 6 = 17; 32 – 9 + 6 = 29; 39 – 9 + 6 = 36; then 46 – 9 + 6 =?

(A) 40   (B) 43   (C) 45   (D) 48

9. Find the division of (32 + 12 + 11 + 5) ÷ 6

(A) 13   (B) 10   (C) 30   (D) 20

10. What is the second one?

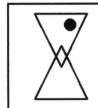   

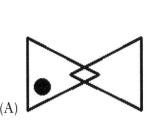 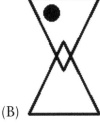 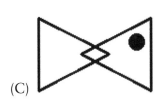 

(A)   (B)   (C)   (D)

11. Find the profit or loss, if Cost Price (CP) is $46.60 and Selling Price (SP) is $49.45?

(A) profit   (B) loss   (C) profit and loss both   (D) none of the above

12. Solve: 6.339 ÷ 3

(A) 5.360   (B) 3.036   (C) 4.046   (D) 2.113

13. Which is the highest fraction?

(A) $2\frac{1}{2}$ (B) $\frac{1.3}{8}$ (C) $1\frac{2}{3}$ (D) $\frac{1}{10}$

14. The lowest common multiple of 12, 21, and 33 is

(A) 924   (B) 440   (C) 1,111   (D) 922

15. Nihar bought a television for $335.90 and sold it for $334.45; find the value of profit or loss:

(A) profit $1.09   (B) loss $0.45   (C) profit $2.47   (D) loss $1.45

16. Which of the following set of signs should be used to replace * in the following?

12 * 2 * 4 < 11 * 3 * 0

(A) ÷, −, −, +   (B) +, −, +, ×   (C) ×, ÷, −, ×   (D) ×, +, +, ×

17. Which of the following expressions has the same value as $14 + \frac{1}{7} \times 12$?

    (A) $\frac{99}{7}$ (B) $\frac{15}{7}$ (C) 15.15   (D) $3\frac{3}{7}$

18. A parallelogram and its angle are shown below.

    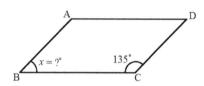

    What is the half of perimeter of the square above?

    (A) 90°   (B) 135°   (C) 30°   (D) 45°

19. Use the coordinate graph below.

    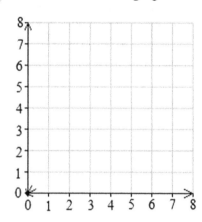

    Alex plotted the following points on the coordinate graph:

    Point A (2, 2); Point B (3, 5); Point D (5, 3)

    Where on the coordinate graph should he plot Point C so that the points form a rhombus with vertices A, B, C, and D, and sides AB, BC, CD, and DA?

    (A) 5, 6   (B) 6, 6   (C) 6, 5   (D) 5, 3

20. Look at the series and find out how many prime numbers are there?
    0, 2, 4, 5, 7, 8, 9, 13, 17, 18, 21, 23

    (A) 10   (B) 12   (C) 6   (D) 5

21. $(2 + 4)^2 = ?$

    (A) 16   (B) 36   (C) 8   (D) 12

22. How many circles are there in the given illusion?

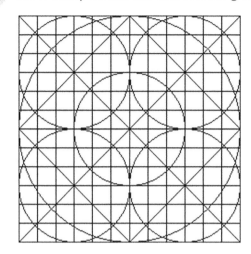

(A) 4 (B) 10 (C) 10 (D) 6

23. Solve: $y + 5x = 20$. Find y where $x = 2$
(A) 20 (B) 15 (C) 10 (D) 25

24. Look at the series 32, 35, 38, _____. What number should come next?
(A) 40 (B) 41 (C) 42 (D) 43

25. Which of following number series is correct multiple series of 17?
(A) 17, 38, 52, 78, 95, 132, 109, 136, 156, 170   (B) 17, 34, 51, 68, 86, 102, 119, 136, 153, 170
(C) 17, 34, 51, 68, 85, 102, 119, 136, 153, 170   (D) 17, 35, 51, 69, 86, 102, 110, 137, 163, 170

26. In the following series, find the number of common multiples of 7 and 13:
81, 91, 150, 182, 235, 273, 314, 364, 455
(A) only three common multiples   (B) only four common multiples
(C) only five common multiples   (D) only six common multiples

27. $\sqrt{y} + \sqrt{49} = 22$, then y is equal to:
(A) 2.77 (B) 9.39 (C) 3.99 (D) 3.87

28. What is the value of the expression: 198 + 227 + 386 − 564?
(A) 472 (B) 356 (C) 247 (D) 250

29. 865.14 ÷ 96.03 = ? (approx.).
(A) 9.00 (B) 0.99 (C) 2.91 (D) 9.01

30. A motorcycle runs 500 km on 30 L of fuel, how many kilometers will it run on 60 L of fuel?

(A) 1,000.20 km   (B) 750.02 km   (C) 1,367.52 km   (D) 1,233.6 km

31. If ∠BCA = 78°, then what is the summation of $x°$ and $y°$?

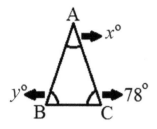

(A) 102°   (B) 24°   (C) 78°   (D) 90°

32. What is the average of the following series?

33, 111, 303, 77, 45

(A) 113.80   (B) 180.55   (C) 565   (D) 33.125

33. Look at the series and find the next number: 3, 6, 9, 12, _____.

(A) 14   (B) 15   (C) 16   (D) 17

34. From this series find the ratio of the prime numbers and compound numbers:

2, 3, 6, 8, 9, 11, 13, 15, 19, 20, 21, 23, 25, 27, 29, 30

(A) 9:7   (B) 8:8   (C) 11:5   (D) 7:9

35. From this series find the ratio of the even numbers and odd numbers:

2, 3, 6, 8, 9, 11, 13, 15, 19, 20, 21, 23, 25, 27, 29, 30

(A) 12:5   (B) 11:6   (C) 5:11   (D) 7:10

36. Look at the picture:

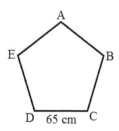

If DC = 65 cm and AB = BC = CD = DE = EA, then find the perimeter of the picture?

(A) 898   (B) 365   (C) 878   (D) 325

37. If ∠BAC = 45°, then find the value of ∠ACX = ?

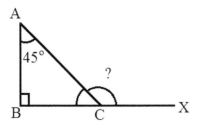

(A) 45°   (B) 180°   (C) 135°   (D) 152°

38. Use the questions below to answer the question.

$5x + 2 = 132$

$11y + 21 = 142$

What is the value of $x \times y = $?

(A) 286   (B) 224   (C) 945   (D) 499

End of section.

If you have any time left, go over the questions in this section only.

Do not start the next section.

You have 25 minutes to answer the 25 questions in the Reading Comprehension and Vocabulary section.

Directions:

This section contains six short reading passages. Each passage is followed by six questions based on its content. Answer the questions following each passage on the basis of what is stated or implied in that passage. You may write in your test booklet.

Questions 1–6

Adults returning to earn their degree should look for colleges with <u>flexible</u> programs and on-campus support services.

Completing a college degree is not an easy feat. It is especially challenging for adult learners, who often <u>juggle</u> family and work responsibilities on top of taking classes.

While there's a "whole social apparatus" set up for students attending college straight out of high school—including college counselors and targeted recruitment programs—adult learners are more on their own, says Terri Taylor, strategy director for innovation and discovery at the Lumina Foundation, an Indiana-based organization that promotes educational access. Even so, more schools are starting to offer tailored support specifically for adult learners.

"Finishing your credentials can be a family-changing decision," Taylor adds. But "it's more of a complex decision for an adult than someone who is 18."

So if you're heading back to college—or even enrolling for the first time as an adult learner—consider the following factors before applying:

Cost.

Support network.

Time constraints.

College support services.

1. The main objective of this passage is

    (A) to give advice to adults returning to college or school

    (B) to inform adults that college is expensive

    (C) to convince adults that college is not necessary

    (D) to discourage adults from going back to college

2. In line 2, what part of speech is the underlined word?

    (A) verb   (B) adjective   (C) noun   (D) adverb

3. In line 2, what does the underlined word mean?

    (A) unwilling to change or compromise

    (B) not able to be changed or adapted to circumstances

    (C) able to be easily modified to respond to altered circumstances or conditions

    (D) not able to be bent; stiff

4. The passage gives enough information to answer which question?

    (A) What universities are best for adults going back to college?

    (B) Which degrees you should not take?

    (C) How much should college cost?

    (D) What are the factors to consider before enrolling in college?

5. What part of speech is the underlined word in line 6?

    (A) verb   (B) noun   (C) adjective   (D) adverb

6. What does the underlined word in line 6 mean?

    (A) cease resistance to an enemy or opponent and submit to their authority

    (B) cope with by adroitly balancing

    (C) give up or hand over (a person, right, or possession), typically on compulsion or demand

    (D) abandon oneself entirely to (a powerful emotion or influence); give in to

Questions 7–12

The median listing price in August was 14% lower than August of 2021 and nearly 42% lower than August of 2019.

Home sellers are getting <u>nervous</u>, as the once hot housing market cools fast.

One in five sellers in August dropped their asking price, according to Realtor.com. A year ago that share was just 11%.

The average home sold for less than its list price for the first time in more than 17 months during the four-week period ended Aug. 28, according to a report by Redfin.

Homes are simply not selling at the <u>breakneck</u> pace they were six months ago when strong demand butted up against tight supply, bidding wars were the norm, and a seller could often get a signed contract in under a weekend. Homes in August sat on the market an average of five days longer than they did a year ago—the first annual increase in time on the market in over two years.

The supply of homes for sale is also rising fast, up nearly 27% from a year ago, even as fewer sellers decide to list. Pending sales in July, which represent signed contracts on existing homes and which are the most recent sales data available, were nearly 20% lower than July 2021, according to the National Association of Realtors.

"For many of today's buyers, the uptick in for-sale home options is taking away the sense of urgency that they felt during the past two years, when inventory was scarce," said Danielle Hale, chief economist for Realtor.com. "As a result of this shift, coupled with higher mortgage rates, competition continued to cool in August, with listing price trends indicating that home shoppers are tightening their purse strings."

7. The main objective of this passage is

   (A) to encourage home shoppers to buy homes now

   (B) to encourage home sellers to stop selling

   (C) to inform the audience that the housing market has slowed down despite prices getting lower

   (D) to educate the audience that it is the best time to buy houses

8. In line 4, what part of speech is the underlined word?

   (A) noun   (B) pronoun   (C) verb   (D) adjective

9. What does the underlined word in line 4 mean?

   (A) not showing or feeling any strong emotion

   (B) peaceful, especially in contrast to recent violent activity

   (C) not disturbed   (D) easily agitated or alarmed; tending to be anxious; highly strung

10. In line 13, what part of speech is the underlined word?

    (A) noun   (B) pronoun   (C) adjective   (D) adverb

11. What does the underlined word in line 13 mean?

    (A) moving or operating, or designed to do so, only at a low speed; not quick or fast

    (B) dangerously or extremely fast   (C) taking a long time to perform a specified action

    (D) not allowing or intended for fast travel

12. How many home sellers have dropped their asking price in August?

    (A) one in five sellers   (B) five sellers in total   (C) 11%   (D) 27%

Questions 13–18

Eating a lot of ultraprocessed foods significantly increases men's risk of colorectal cancer and can lead to heart disease and early death in both men and women, according to two new, large-scale studies of people in the United States and Italy published Wednesday in British medical journal *The BMJ*.

Ultraprocessed foods include prepackaged soups, sauces, frozen pizza, ready-to-eat meals and pleasure foods such as hot dogs, sausages, french fries, sodas, store-bought cookies, cakes, candies, doughnuts, ice cream and many more.

"Literally hundreds of studies link ultra-processed foods to obesity, cancer, cardiovascular disease, and overall mortality," said Marion Nestle, the Paulette Goddard professor emerita of nutrition, food studies and public health at New York University and author of numerous books on food politics and marketing, including 2015's "Soda Politics: Taking on Big Soda (and Winning)."

"These two studies continue the consistency: Ultraprocessed foods are <u>unambiguously</u> associated with an increased risk for chronic disease," said Nestle, who was not involved in either study.

The US-based study <u>examined</u> the diets of over 200,000 men and women for up to 28 years and found a link between ultraprocessed foods and colorectal cancer—the third most diagnosed cancer in the US—in men, but not women.

Processed and ultraprocessed meats, such as ham, bacon, salami, hotdogs, beef jerky and corned beef, have long been associated with a higher risk of bowel cancer in both men and women, according to the World Health Organization, American Cancer Society and the American Institute for Cancer Research.

The new study, however, found that all types of ultraprocessed foods played a role to some degree.

13. The main objective of this passage is

(A) to inform the audience that there is no link between processed foods and cancer

(B) to convince readers to stock their pantry with processed foods since they are convenient and cheaper

(C) to cite the benefits of consuming processed foods

(D) to educate the audience the link of ultraprocessed foods with cancer and early death

14. In line 23, what part of speech is the underlined word?

(A) noun　(B) verb　(C) adverb　(D) adjective

15. In line 23, what is the meaning of the underlined word?

(A) so as to be open to more than one interpretation

(B) in a manner that is not open to more than one interpretation

(C) to be open to doubt or uncertainty　(D) not easy to see, hear, or understand

16. In line 27, what part of speech is the underlined word?

(A) verb   (B) adverb   (C) preposition   (D) adjective

17. In line 27, what is the meaning of the underlined word?

(A) inspect in detail to determine their nature or condition   (B) put in place or erect quickly

(C) firmly decide   (D) open to more than one interpretation; inexactness

18. The passage gives enough information to answer which question?

(A) Where should I buy my processed foods?   (B) What are ultraprocessed foods?

(C) Until what age can I eat ultraprocessed foods?   (D) How much does a pack of bacon cost?

Questions 19–25

Jenna Goldman said she was out on a run with her now-husband two years ago when she started feeling like she was getting a migraine.

"In my right eye, there was some vision stuff happening, like a typical ocular migraine," Goldman, 28, told "Good Morning America," referring to a type of migraine headache that temporarily causes vision loss in one eye, according to the American Optometric Association.

Goldman, of New York, said she had suffered from ocular migraines since the age of 21, so when symptoms struck during her run, she went home and began to treat it as she usually did, with deep breaths, a wet cloth on her face and over-the-counter pain medication.

This time though, Goldman said she continued to feel worse and soon felt numbness in her body and had difficulty speaking.

Goldman's husband took her to a local hospital, where she said doctors first treated her for a migraine but ultimately diagnosed her as suffering a stroke.

"The doctor said, 'Jenna, you're going to need to get your parents or your fiancé to hop on the phone because you're not going to be able to comprehend what I'm going to tell you,' and she said that I had a stroke," Goldman recalled. "I didn't even know what that meant, but just knew that it was really bad."

Goldman said that in addition to her shock that she, as a healthy 20-something, would be impacted by a stroke, she was also surprised to learn from doctors that the hormonal birth control she had taken since the age of 17 may have added to her stroke risk.

Experiencing migraines with aura, of which ocular migraines are included, slightly increases a woman's risk of stroke, according to the American Migraine Foundation. Taking hormonal birth control can also slightly increase a woman's risk of stroke.

19. The main objective of this passage is

(A) to convince women to stop taking birth control pills

(B) to suggest which birth control pills are the best

(C) to learn from Jenna's experience the importance of asking your doctor the risk of taking birth control pills

(D) to highlight that birth control pills are not good for your health

20. In line 25, what part of speech is the underlined word?

(A) noun (B) pronoun (C) adjective (D) verb

21. In line 25, what does the underlined word mean?

(A) join something quickly (B) get off of something

(C) get into a vehicle (D) to move by a quick springy leap

22. In line 27, what part of speech is the underlined word?

(A) verb (B) adverb (C) noun (D) pronoun

23. In line 27, what does the underlined word mean?

(A) discover or perceive by chance or unexpectedly (B) grasp mentally; understand

(C) take into one's possession or control by force (D) resolve or reach an agreement about

24. How old was Jenna when she started taking hormonal birth control?

(A) 20-something (B) 17 (C) 21 (D) 28

25. At what age did Jenna start to suffer from ocular migraines?

(A) 20-something (B) 17 (C) 21 (D) 28

End of section.

If you have any time left, go over the questions in this section only.

Do not start the next section.

You have 30 minutes to answer the 30 questions in the Mathematics Achievement Section.

Each question is followed by four suggested answers. Read each question and then decide which one of the four suggested answers is best.

Find the row of spaces on your document that has the same number as the question. In this row, mark the space having the same letter as the answer you have chosen. You may write in your test booklet.

SAMPLE QUESTION:

Which of the numbers below is not a factor of 364?

(A) 13
(B) 20
(C) 26
(D) 91

The correct answer is 20, so circle B is darkened.

<u>Sample Answer</u>

A ● C D

---

1. Shown below is a plan for a grocery store's building. Here EF is 2 km, and all sides are same.

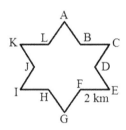

   According to the grocery store's plan, what will be the perimeter (*P*) of the store?

   (A) 24 km   (B) 32 km   (C) 50 km   (D) 60 km

2. Look at the series: 121, 132, 143, 154, 165, 176, _____, ... *n*. What will be the number to fill the blank?

   (A) 209   (B) 198   (C) 176   (D) 187

3. The sum of ages of father and son is 45. What will be the sum of ages of them after 25 years?

   (A) 70 years   (B) 95 years   (C) 50 years   (D) sum of the ages will be same

4. If (441 ÷ ■) × 21 = 1,323, what number does ■ stands for?

   (A) 21   (B) –17   (C) 7   (D) 14

5. Which function is equivalent to 121.97?

(A) $97\dfrac{116}{100}$ (B) $\dfrac{1,160}{1,000}$ (C) $121\dfrac{97}{100}$ (D) 12

6. Use the number sequence to answer the question.

2, 4, _____, _____, 10 ...

(A) 6, 8   (B) 5, 6   (C) 6, 7   (D) 8, 9

7. Lumi sold 12,100 goods from her shop. The below table shows the results.

Items	Number of Goods
Cotton balls	3,060
Leather bags	2,300
Flower vases	2,000
Pencil boxes	2,240
Flowers	2,500

What is the difference between flowers and pencil boxes?

(A) –260   (B) 233   (C) –233   (D) 260

8. Which of the following is equal to $9.03 \times \dfrac{58}{189}$?

(A) $\dfrac{9.03 \times 58}{18,900}$ (B) $\dfrac{903 \times 58}{18,900}$ (C) $\dfrac{903 \times 58}{100 \times 18,900}$ (D) $\dfrac{903 \times 58}{189}$

9. Which of the following numbers is divisible by 5 with a remainder 3?

(A) 374   (B) 618   (C) 741   (D) 300

10. What is difference between $(657 \div 3)$ and $\dfrac{2}{12}$?

(A) 215.83   (B) 261.12   (C) 218.83   (D) 218.12

11. $6^2 + 8^2 =$

(A) 13^2 (B) 12^2 (C) 11^2 (D) 10^2

12. Which of the following numbers is a multiple of 81?

(A) 6,561   (B) 6,051   (C) 6,305   (D) 6,230

13. What is the multiplication of 36.56 and 7.5?

(A) 274.20   (B) 336.01   (C) 114.07   (D) 160.16

14. What is the value of the expression 9,782.03 – 427.49?

(A) 5,409.03 (B) 9,354.54 (C) 6,509.28 (D) 558.04

15. The multiplication of two numbers is 1,296. If one number is 108, what is the second one?

(A) 36 (B) 12 (C) 6 (D) 3

16. What is the value of the expression?

$(42 + 13 - 11 - 13 \times 2) \times (34 \times 17)$

(A) 36,302 (B) 10,404 (C) 14,150 (D) 13,000

17. The summation of two numbers is 3,598. If one number is 2,659, then what is another one?

(A) 586 (B) 492 (C) 939 (D) 984

18. In a primary school there are only six classes. Each class has four sections and each class has been allotted one room for every section. How many rooms are there in the school?

(A) 24 (B) 36 (C) 16 (D) 12

19. If $x^4 = 625$, then the value of x = ?

(A) 3 (B) 6 (C) 4 (D) 5

20. The sum of the age of mother and daughter is 55. Mother's age is 40. What is the age of daughter after 12 years?

(A) 25 years (B) 75 years (C) 15 years (D) 25 years

21. Use the set of numbers shown to answer the question.

{12, 22, 36, 46, 60, ...}

Which describes this set of numbers?

(A) multiples of 12 (B) odd numbers (C) even numbers (D) decimal numbers

22. What is the value of the expression: $(1,000 \div 25 \times 9 + 240) \div 5$?

(A) 120 (B) 48.89 (C) 600 (D) 50

23. Which number is divisible by 15 without a remainder and also 19?

(A) 280 (B) 570 (C) 244 (D) none of the above

24. What is the standard form of eighteen lakhs fifty-seven?

(A) 1,800,057 (B) 1,857,000 (C) 5,718,000 (D) invalid number

25. If angle ∠BCA = 45° of a triangle, what is the summation of ∠ABC and ∠BAC ?

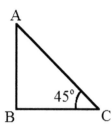

(A) 135° (B) 180° (C) 90° (D) 45°

26. What is the average of this series?

11, 11, 12, 13, 13, 15, 16

(A) 13 (B) 25 (C) 30 (D) 45

27. Miss. Jenney has 100 boxes of pens. Each box contains 15 pens. If X represents the total number of pens, which equation would tell her how many pens she has?

(A) $100 \times 15 = X$ (B) $X + 15 = 100$ (C) $1,500 = \dfrac{X}{17}$ (D) $X = \dfrac{1,500}{15}$

28. The below graph shows the number of burgers sold at a bakery bake sale.

Hours since Start of Sale	Burgers Sold
1	⊖ ⊖ ⊖ ⊖ ⊖
2	⊖ ⊖ ⊖ ⊖ ⊖ ⊖ ⊖ ⊖
3	⊖ ⊖ ⊖ ⊖ ⊖ ⊖ ⊖ ⊖
4	⊖ ⊖ ⊖ ⊖ ⊖ ⊖ ⊖ ⊖ ⊖ ⊖ ⊖ ⊖ ⊖ ⊖ ⊖
5	⊖ ⊖ ⊖ ⊖ ⊖ ⊖ ⊖ ⊖ ⊖ ⊖

⊖ = 18 burgers sold

How many burgers were sold at the bake sale?

(A) 450 (B) 900 (C) 455 (D) 810

29. If the radius of a circle is 13 m, then what is the area (A) of the circle, where $\pi = \dfrac{22}{7}$?

(A) 532.55 (B) 200.36 (C) 531.14 (D) none of the above

30. Which of the following number is divisible by 17 with a remainder 3?

(A) 3,074 (B) 6,180 (C) 3,142 (D) 2,060

End of section.

If you have any time left, go over the questions in this section only.
Do not start the next section.

Essay Topic Sheet

The directions for the Essay portion of the ISEE are printed in the box below. Use the pre-lined pages on pages 145 and 146 for this part of the Practice Test.

You will have 30 minutes to plan and write an essay on the topic printed on the other side of this page. **Do not write on another topic. An essay on another topic is not acceptable.**

The essay is designed to give you an opportunity to show how well you can write. You should try to express your thoughts clearly. How well you write is much more important than how much you write, but you need to say enough for a reader to understand what you mean.

You will probably want to write more than a short paragraph. You should also be aware that a copy of your essay will be sent to each school that will be receiving your test results. You are to write only in the appropriate section of the answer sheet. Please write or print so that your writing may be read by someone who is not familiar with your handwriting.

You may make notes and plan your essay on the reverse side of the page. Allow enough time to copy the final form onto your answer sheet. You must copy the essay topic onto your answer sheet, in the box provided.

Please remember to write only the final draft of the essay on your answer sheet and to write it in blue or black pen. Again, you may use cursive writing, or you may print. Only pages 145 and 146 will be sent to the schools.

Directions continue on the next page.

REMINDER: Please write this essay topic on the first few lines of your answer sheet.

Essay Topic

Among the colors of the rainbow, which color is your favorite? Why did you choose this color?

- Only write on this essay question
- Only pages 145 and 146 will be sent to the schools
- Only write in blue or black pen

NOTES

_____

_____

_____

_____

_____

_____

_____

_____

_____

_____

_____

_____

_____

_____

_____

_____

_____

_____

_____

STUDENT NAME _____ GRADE APPLYING FOR _____

Use a blue or black ballpoint pen to write the final draft of your essay on this sheet.

You must write your essay topic in this space.

_____

_____

_____

Use specific details in your response

_____

_____

_____

_____

_____

_____

_____

_____

_____

_____

_____

_____

_____

_____

_____

_____

_____

_____

End of section.

If you have any time left, go over the questions in this section only.

ANSWER KEY

Verbal Reasoning

1. A	7. B	13. D	19. C	25. C	31. A
2. B	8. A	14. D	20. D	26. A	32. B
3. C	9. C	15. A	21. B	27. B	33. C
4. D	10. C	16. A	22. A	28. A	34. D
5. D	11. B	17. C	23. A	29. C	
6. C	12. B	18. A	24. B	30. D	

1. The correct answer is (A). Civic means relating to a city or town, especially its administration; municipal. Synonyms are public, civil, and local. Sample: "civic and business leaders."

2. The correct answer is (B). Coincidence is defined as a remarkable concurrence of events or circumstances without apparent causal connection. Synonyms are accident, chance, and fate. Sample: "They met by coincidence."

3. The correct answer is (C). To commend means to praise formally or officially. Synonyms are praise, compliment, and applaud. Sample: "He was commended by the judge for his courageous actions."

4. The correct answer is (D). Compact means closely and neatly packed together; dense. Synonyms are dense, tight, and firm. Sample: "a compact cluster of houses"

5. The correct answer is (D). To consent means to give permission for something to happen. Synonyms are to allow, accept, and approve. Sample: "He consented to a search by a detective."

6. The correct answer is (C). Conspicuous means attracting notice or attention. Synonyms are clear, visible, and noticeable. Sample: "He showed conspicuous bravery."

7. The correct answer is (B). To deluge means to inundate with a great quantity of something. Synonyms are flood, overload, and overwhelm. Sample: "He has been deluged with offers of work."

8.   The correct answer is (A). To deplete is to use up the supply or resources of. Synonyms are exhaust, consume, and expend. Sample: "reservoirs have been depleted by years of drought"

9.   The correct answer is (C). Dense means closely compacted in substance. Synonyms are thick, heavy, and concentrated. Sample: "dense volcanic rock"

10. The correct answer is (C). To devise is to plan or invent (a complex procedure, system, or mechanism) by careful thought. Devise is a verb. Synonyms are to formulate, design, and invent. Sample: "a training program should be devised."

11. The correct answer is (B). To deteriorate means to become progressively worse. Synonyms are to worsen, degenerate, and decay. Sample: "relations between the countries had deteriorated sharply"

12. The correct answer is (B). To diminish is to make or become less. Synonyms are decrease, decline, and reduce. Sample: "a tax whose purpose is to diminish spending"

13. The correct answer is (D). To dismantle is to take (a machine or structure) to pieces. Synonyms are to deconstruct, disassemble, and destroy. Sample: "The engines were dismantled, and the bits piled into a heap."

14. The correct answer is (D). To dissolve means to (of something abstract, especially a feeling) disappear. Synonyms are to vanish, evaporate, and disperse. Sample: "my courage dissolved"

15. The correct answer is (A). A drawback is a feature that renders something less acceptable, a disadvantage or problem. Synonyms are disadvantage, catch, and downside. Sample: "The main drawback of modernization is pollution."

16. The correct answer is (A). Drastic means likely to have a strong or far-reaching effect; radical and extreme. Synonyms are extreme, serious, and desperate. Sample: "a drastic reduction of staffing levels"

17. The correct answer is (C). Edible means fit or suitable to be eaten. Synonyms are consumable, palatable, and digestible. Sample: "The shrub has small edible berries."

18. The correct answer is (A). Break in is a phrasal verb which means to interrupt. In this sentence the radio station interrupted the regular program or the current segment to make an announcement.

19. The correct answer is (C). Call something off is a phrasal verb which means to cancel something. In this sentence, the bride is about to cancel the wedding after finding out that the groom doesn't want to move out from his parents' house.

20. The correct answer is (D). Chip in is a phrasal verb which means to help. In this sentence, the speaker expected the other person to help when the other person volunteered for the community outreach program.

21. The correct answer is (B). Count on is a phrasal verb which means to rely on someone. In this sentence, mom is relying on the other person to watch over the house while they are away on vacation.

22. The correct answer is (A). Cut back on something is a phrasal verb which means to consume less. In this sentence, the doctor recommended to consume less unhealthy fats.

23. The correct answer is (A). Do something over is a phrasal verb which means to do again. In this sentence, the students had to do their projects again.

24. The correct answer is (B). Do away with something is a phrasal verb which means to discard. In this sentence, the speaker is saying that it is time to discard the outgrown clothes.

25. The correct answer is (C). Dress up is a phrasal verb which means to wear nice clothing. In this sentence, the subject quickly wore nice clothing and out on her fine jewelry for dinner.

26. The correct answer is (A). Grow out of something is a phrasal verb which means get too big for. In this sentence, the speaker's dad bought a new pair of shoes to replace the pair he got too big for.

27. The correct answer is (B). Bare means (of a person or part of the body) not clothed or covered.

28. The correct answer is (A). Bear is a verb which means carry the weight of, support.

29. The correct answer is (C). To incite is to urge or persuade (someone) to act in a violent or unlawful way.

30. The correct answer is (D). Insight means a deep understanding of a person or thing.

31. The correct answer is (A). Real is defined as (of a substance or thing) not imitation or artificial; genuine.

32. The correct answer is (B). Reel is a cylinder on which film, wire, thread, or other flexible materials can be wound.

33. The correct answer is (C). A tail is the hindmost part of an animal.

34. The correct answer is (D). A tale is a fictitious or true narrative or story, especially one that is imaginatively recounted.

Quantitative Reasoning

1. D	11. A	21. B	31. A
2. B	12. D	22. D	32. A
3. A	13. A	23. C	33. B
4. C	14. A	24. B	34. D
5. A	15. D	25. C	35. C
6. C	16. A	26. C	36. D
7. B	17. A	27. D	37. C
8. B	18. D	28. C	38. A
9. B	19. B	29. D	
10. D	20. C	30. A	

1. The correct answer is (D). We know the perimeter of the triangle is (P) = 3a (here a = side).

   As this is an equilateral triangle.

   So, perimeter of the triangle = 3a = 3 × 6 km = 18 km.

2. The correct answer is (B). [{(222 D 11) B 19} C 9] A 31 = [{(222 ÷ 11) + 19} × 9] − 31 = [{2 + 19} × 9] − 31 = [21 × 9] − 31 = 189 − 31 = 158.

3. The correct answer is (A). We know ascending order means the series arranged from lowest to highest. So, assemble 20, 38, 9, 16, 38 in ascending we get 9, 16, 20, 36, 38.

4. The correct answer is (C).

$$\left(\frac{1}{7}+\frac{5}{7}\right)-\left(\frac{1}{5}+\frac{2}{5}\right)=\left(1+\frac{5}{7}\right)-\left(1+\frac{2}{5}\right). = \frac{6}{7}-\frac{3}{5}=30-\frac{21}{35}$$

$$=\frac{9}{35} \text{ (Answer).}$$

5. The correct answer is (A).

   24 ÷ 4 × (6 − 3) − 24 ÷ 4 (6 − 3) = 24 ÷ 4 × 3 − 24 ÷ 4 of 3 = 6 × 3 − 24 ÷ 12

   = 6 × 3 − 2 = 18 − 2 = 16 (Answer).

6. The correct answer is (C).

   11 = 1 × 11

   55 = 1 × 5 × 11

   121 = 1 × 11 × 11

   So, the greatest common factor of 11, 55, and 121 is 1 and 11.

7. The correct answer is (B). G.C.D. of 13, 65, 78, and 104 is 26.

8. The correct answer is (B).

   20 – 9 + 6 = 17;

   32 – 9 + 6 = 29;

   39 – 9 + 6 = 36;

   then 46 – 9 + 6 = 43.

9. The correct answer is (B). (32 + 12 + 11 + 5) ÷ 6 = 60 ÷ 6 = 10.

10. The correct answer is (D). The triangle rotates clockwise. So, option "D" is true.

11. The correct answer is (A).

    CP = $46.60 and SP = $49.45.

    Here, SP > CP.

    So, it is a profit.

12. The correct answer is (D). 6.339 ÷ 3 = 2.113.

13. The correct answer is (A).

    L.C.M. of all denominators is 240

    So, $2\frac{1}{2} = \frac{5 \times 120}{2 \times 120} = \frac{600}{240} = 600$

    $\frac{1.3}{8} = \frac{13}{8 \times 10} = \frac{13 \times 3}{80 \times 3} = \frac{39}{240} = 39$

    $1\frac{2}{3} = \frac{5 \times 80}{3 \times 80} = \frac{400}{240} = 400$

    $\frac{1}{10} = \frac{1 \times 24}{10 \times 24} = \frac{24}{240} = 24$

    So, the highest fraction is $2\frac{1}{2}$.

14. The correct answer is (A).

Prime factorization of the numbers:

$12 = 2 \times 2 \times 3$

$21 = 3 \times 7$

$33 = 3 \times 11$

LCM(12, 21, 33)

$= 2 \times 2 \times 3 \times 7 \times 11$

$= 924$

15. The correct answer is (D).

CP = \$335.90 and SP = \$334.45.

Here, CP > SP.

So, it is a loss.

$\therefore$ Loss = CP – SP = 335.90 – 334.45 = 1.45

16. The correct answer is (A). $12 * 2 * 4 < 11 * 3 * 0 = 12 \div 2 - 4 < 11 - 3 + 4 \Rightarrow 0 < 8$.

17. The correct answer is (A). $14 + \dfrac{1}{7} \times 12 = 14 + \dfrac{1}{7} = \dfrac{98+1}{7} = \dfrac{99}{7}$.

18. The correct answer is (D). We know the opposite angles of a parallelogram are equal.

So, $\angle BCD = \angle BAD = 135°$...(i)

And $\angle ABC = \angle CDA = x°$

Also we know the summation of all angles of a parallelogram is 360°.

$\therefore \ \angle ABC + \angle BCD + \angle DBA + \angle DAB = 360°$

$\Rightarrow x° + 135° + x° + 135° = 360°$

$\Rightarrow 2x° = 360° - 270°$

$\Rightarrow x° = 90° \div 2 = 45°$ (Answer).

19. The correct answer is (B).

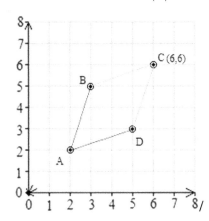

20. The correct answer is (C). 0 is neither prime number nor compound number.

So, the prime numbers according to the given series are 2, 5, 7, 13, 17, and 23.

∴ Only six prime numbers are there.

21. The correct answer is (B). $(2 + 4)^2 = 6^2 = 36$.

22. The correct answer is (D).

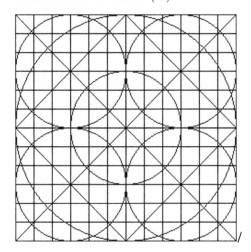

There are six circles.

23. The correct answer is (C).

$y + 5x = 20$

$\Rightarrow y = 20 - 5 \times 2$ ($x = 2$ given)

$\Rightarrow y = 20 - 10 = 10$.

24. The correct answer is (B). 32 + 3 = 35; 35 + 3 = 38; 38 + 3 = 41.

25. The correct answer is (C). The multiplication table of 17 is 17, 34, 51, 68, 85, 102, 119, 136, 153, 170, and so on.

26. The correct answer is (C). 81, <u>91</u>, 150, <u>182</u>, 235, <u>273</u>, 314, <u>364</u>, <u>455</u>: in this series, only the underlined numbers are divisible by 7 and 13 both.

27. The correct answer is (D). $\sqrt{y} + \sqrt{49} = 22 \Rightarrow \sqrt{y} = 22 - 7; \Rightarrow y = 3.87$ (approx.).

28. The correct answer is (C). 198 + 227 + 386 − 564 = 247.

29. The correct answer is (D). 865.14 ÷ 96.03 = 9.009... = 9.01 (approx.).

30. The correct answer is (A).

30 L $\Rightarrow$ 500 km

∴ 1 L $\Rightarrow$ (500/30) km = 16.67 km (approx.)

∴ 60 L $\Rightarrow$ (60 × 16.67) km = 1,000.20 km.

31. The correct answer is (A).

We know the total of all angles of a triangle is 180° and the opposite angles of an isosceles triangle are equal.

Here, ∠BCA = 78°

∴ ∠ABC = $y°$ also 78°

So, ∠CAB = 180° − (∠BCA + ∠ABC)

$\Rightarrow x° = 180° − (78° + 78°) = 180° − 156° = 24°.$

∴ $x° + y° = 24° + 78° = 102°.$

32. The correct answer is (A). (33 + 111 + 303 + 77 + 45) ÷ 6 = 569 ÷ 5 = 113.80.

33. The correct answer is (B).

3 $\Rightarrow$ 3 + 2 + 1 = 6

6 $\Rightarrow$ 6 + 2 + 1 = 9

9 $\Rightarrow$ 9 + 2 + 1 = 12

12 $\Rightarrow$ 12 + 2 + 1 = <u>15</u>.

34. The correct answer is (D).

    According to the series—

    (i) Prime numbers are 2, 3, 11, 13, 19, 23, 29

    (ii) Compound numbers are 6, 8, 9, 15, 20, 21, 25, 27, 30

    ∴ The ratio will be = 7:9.

35. The correct answer is (C).

    According to the series, the even numbers are 2, 6, 8, 20, and 30

    And the odd numbers are 3, 9, 11, 13, 15, 19, 21, 23, 25, 27, and 29

    ∴ Even Number:Odd Number = 5:11.

36. The correct answer is (D). The perimeter of the picture is (65 cm × 5 cm) = 325 cm.

37. The correct answer is (C). We know that the summation of all angles of a triangle is 180° and the measurement of a straight angle is 180°.

    Here, ∠BCX = 180°, ΔABC = 180°, where ∠BAC = 45° and ∠ABC is a right angle, therefore 90°

    So, ∠BCA = 180° – (∠ABC + ∠BAC) = 180° – (90° + 45°) = 45°

    Therefore, ∠ACX = ∠BCX – ∠ACB = 180° – 45° = 135°.

38. The correct answer is (A).

    $5x + 2 = 132 \Rightarrow 5x = 132 - 2 \Rightarrow x = \dfrac{130}{5} = 26$

    $11y + 21 = 142 \Rightarrow 11y = 142 - 21 \Rightarrow y = \dfrac{121}{11} = 11;$

    ∴ $x \times y = 26 \times 11 = 286.$

Reading Comprehension and Vocabulary

1. A	6. B	11. B	16. A	21. A
2. B	7. C	12. A	17. A	22. A
3. C	8. D	13. D	18. B	23. B
4. D	9. D	14. C	19. C	24. B
5. A	10. C	15. B	20. D	25. C

1. The correct answer is (A). The passage is about the things to consider when going back to college as an adult. See lines 1–3, 22–28.

2. The correct answer is (B). Flexible is an adjective which means able to be easily modified to respond to altered circumstances or conditions. Sample: "flexible forms of retirement"

3. The correct answer is (C). Flexible is an adjective which means able to be easily modified to respond to altered circumstances or conditions. Sample: "flexible forms of retirement"

4. The correct answer is (D). See lines 22–28.

5. The correct answer is (A). Juggle is a verb which means cope with by adroitly balancing. Sample: "She works full time, juggling her career with raising children."

6. The correct answer is (B). Juggle is a verb which means cope with by adroitly balancing. Sample: "She works full time, juggling her career with raising children."

7. The correct answer is (C). The passage presents statistics on how the housing market performance is recently. See lines 1–2 and the rest of the passage indicating percentages of how much asking prices dropped, how much supply of homes for sale increased even as fewer sellers list, and how much pending sales lowered.

8. The correct answer is (D). Nervous is an adjective which means easily agitated or alarmed; tending to be anxious; highly strung. Sample: "staying in the house on her own made her nervous"

9. The correct answer is (D). Nervous is an adjective which means easily agitated or alarmed; tending to be anxious; highly strung. Sample: "staying in the house on her own made her nervous"

10. The correct answer is (C). Breakneck is an adjective which means dangerously or extremely fast. Sample: "He drove at breakneck speed."

11. The correct answer is (B). Breakneck is an adjective which means dangerously or extremely fast. Sample: "He drove at breakneck speed."

12. The correct answer is (A). See lines 6–7.

13. The correct answer is (D). The passage discusses how ultraprocessed foods have been proven by studies to increase risk of cancer and early death in both men and women. See lines 1–4.

14. The correct answer is (C). Unambiguously is an adverb which modifies the verb associated in this line. It means in a manner that is not open to more than one interpretation. Sample: "She answered questions clearly and unambiguously."

15. The correct answer is (B). Unambiguously is an adverb which modifies the verb associated in this line. It means in a manner that is not open to more than one interpretation. Sample: "She answered questions clearly and unambiguously."

16. The correct answer is (A). The word examined is the past tense of the verb examine which means to inspect (someone or something) in detail to determine their nature or condition; investigate thoroughly. Sample: "A doctor examined me and said I might need a caesarean."

17. The correct answer is (A). The word examined is the past tense of the verb examine which means to inspect (someone or something) in detail to determine their nature or condition; investigate thoroughly. Sample: "A doctor examined me and said I might need a caesarean."

18. The correct answer is (B). See lines 8–12, 32–34.

19. The correct answer is (C). The passage is about Jenna Goldman's stroke experience and finding out that hormonal birth control she had taken since the age of 17 may have added to her stroke risk.

20. The correct answer is (D). Hop on is a phrasal verb which is an informal way of saying to jump onto something or to join something quickly.

21. The correct answer is (A). Hop on is a phrasal verb which is an informal way of saying to jump onto something or to join something quickly.

22. The correct answer is (A). Comprehend is a verb which means to grasp mentally; understand. Sample: "He couldn't comprehend her reasons for marrying Lovat."

23. The correct answer is (B). Comprehend is a verb which means to grasp mentally; understand. Sample: "He couldn't comprehend her reasons for marrying Lovat."

24. The correct answer is (B). See line 35.

25. The correct answer is (C). See line 12.

Mathematics Achievement

1. A	11. D	21. C
2. D	12. A	22. A
3. B	13. A	23. B
4. C	14. B	24. A
5. C	15. B	25. A
6. A	16. B	26. A
7. D	17. C	27. A
8. B	18. A	28. D
9. B	19. D	29. C
10. C	20. D	30. D

1. The correct answer is (A). Perimeter = Number of sides × range.
    There are 12 sides
    $\therefore P = 12 \times 2$ km = 24 km.

2. The correct answer is (D). $(11 \times 11) = 121$, $(11 \times 12) = 132$, $(11 \times 13) = 143$, $(11 \times 14) = 154$, (11×15)
    $= 165$, $(11 \times 16) = 176$, $(11 \times 17) = \underline{187}$ ..., n.

3. The correct answer is (B).

    The sum of the ages of father and son is 45 (now).

    After 25 years both of their ages will increase by 25 years.

    So, the sum of the ages of father and son after 25 years will be: $45 + (25 + 25) = 95$ years.

4. The correct answer is (C). $(441 \div \blacksquare) \times 21 = 1{,}323$. Let $x = \blacksquare$;
    $\dfrac{441}{\blacksquare} \times 21 = 1{,}323; x = \dfrac{1{,}323}{441 \times 21}; \therefore x = 7.$

5. The correct answer is (C). $121.97 = \dfrac{12{,}197}{100} \therefore 12{,}197 \div 100 = 121\dfrac{97}{100}.$

6. The correct answer is (A). The given series is an even series, so the answer will be 6 and 8.

7. The correct answer is (D). The difference between flowers and pencil boxes is $(2{,}500 - 2{,}240) = 260$.

8. The correct answer is (B). $9.03 \times \dfrac{58}{189}$, we can write it in this way: $\dfrac{903 \times 58}{100 \times 189}$ or $\dfrac{903 \times 58}{18{,}900}$.

9. The correct answer is (B). Among the options only 618 is divisible by 5 and 3 both. So, it is the answer.

10. The correct answer is (C). The difference between $(657 \div 3)$ and $\dfrac{2}{12}$ is = $\dfrac{2,628-2}{12} = \dfrac{2,626}{12} = 218.83$ (approx.).

11. The correct answer is (D). $6^2 + 8^2 = 36 + 64 = 100 = 10^2$

12. The correct answer is (A). The multiple of 81 is 6,561.

13. The correct answer is (A). $36.56 \times 7.5 = 274.20$.

14. The correct answer is (B). $9,782.03 - 427.49 = 9,354.54$.

15. The correct answer is (B). Second number is $(1,296 \div 108) = 12$.

16. The correct answer is (B). $(42 + 13 - 11 - 13 \times 2) \times (34 \times 17) = (42 + 13 - 11 - 26) \times 578 = 18 \times 578 = 10,404$.

17. The correct answer is (C). Another one is $(3,598 - 2,659) = 939$.

18. The correct answer is (A). (Number of Classes × Number of Sections) = $(6 \times 4) = 24$ rooms.

19. The correct answer is (D). $x^4 = 625 \Rightarrow x^4 = 5^4 \therefore x = 5$.

20. The correct answer is (D). Mother + Daughter = 55

    40 + Daughter = 55

    ∴ Daughter = 55 – 40 = 15 years

    After 10 years daughter's age will be (15 + 10) = 25 years.

21. The correct answer is (C). 12, 22, 36, 46, 60, …. is the series of even numbers.

22. The correct answer is (A). $(1,000 \div 25 \times 9 + 240) \div 5 = 120$.

23. The correct answer is (B). Five hundred and seventy is divisible by 15 and 19 both without any remainder.

24. The correct answer is (A). The standard form of eighteen lakhs fifty-seven is 1,800,087.

25. The correct answer is (A). We know the opposite angles of a right-angle triangle are equal one is 90°.

    So, if ∠BCA = 45°, then as per the rule ∠CAB has same value 45° and ∠ABC = 90°.

    ∴ ∠ABC + ∠ACB = 90° + 45° = 135°.

26.   The correct answer is (A). (11 + 11 + 12 + 13 + 13 + 15 + 16) ÷ 7 = 13.

27.   The correct answer is (A). There are 100 boxes and each box has 15 pens (100 × 15).

28.   The correct answer is (D). The total number of burgers sold = 45 × 18 = 810.

29.   The correct answer is (C). We know the area of a circle is $= \pi r^2$.

Here $\pi = \dfrac{22}{7}$, and $r = 13$ m.

Therefore, $A = \pi r^2 = \dfrac{22}{7} \times 13^2 = 531.1428$ sq. m $= 531.14$ sq. m (approx.).

30.   The correct answer is (D). Among the options only 2,060 is divisible by 17 and 3 both. So, it is the answer.

Sample Essay Response

Among the colors of the rainbow, my favorite color is red. I have a warm undertone and red suits me well. Red is such a vibrant color and is often associated with strong symbolic meanings in many cultures.

Being an Asian, I grew up wearing red on birthdays and holidays because they symbolize luck and success in our culture. Red is the color of blood which can be the reason why the color is often associated with love. They say you instantly look more attractive to the opposite sex when you wear red, whether a dress or your lipstick. In China, it is traditional for the bride to wear red during the wedding to wish for a fulfilling marriage.

Red is also associated with anger, war, courage and vigor. All these symbolic meanings have in common is that they all require passion and energy. Psychology has studied the effects of color red on the human brain. Red increases enthusiasm and stimulates energy while increasing blood pressure and heart rate. It also calls someone's attention for action, increases confidence and provides a sense of security and protection against fear and anxiety.

How does your culture perceive this color?

For the ISEE, the most commonly referenced score is the stanine score. Check out the four steps to calculating stanine scores.

Step 1: The Raw Score

The first step in scoring is calculating a raw score. This is quite simple.

Students receive one point for each correct answer and no points for incorrect answers or unanswered questions.

Tip: Because there is no score penalty for incorrect answers or unanswered questions, be sure to answer every single question! Answering all of the questions can only increase your chances of a higher score.

Step 2: The Scaled Score

Once a raw score has been calculated for each section, it is converted into a scaled score.

This conversion adjusts for the variation in difficulty between different tests. Thus, a lower raw score on a harder test could give you the same scaled score as a higher raw score on an easier test. This process is called equating.

The scaled score for each section ranges from 760 to 940.

Step 3: The Percentile Score

Next, the percentile score for each section is calculated.

Percentiles compare a student's scaled score to all other same-grade students from the past three years. This is important to understand because the ISEE is taken by students in a range of grades. The Upper Level ISEE, for instance, is taken by students applying to grades 9–12; however, the percentile score is based only on the performance of other students applying to the same grade. Thus, a student applying to 9th grade will not be compared to a student applying to 12th grade.

Here's an example to help understand percentile scores: scoring in the 40th percentile indicates that a student scored the same or higher than 40% of students in the same grade but lower than 59% of students.

Step 4: The Stanine Score

Finally, the percentile is converted into a stanine score.

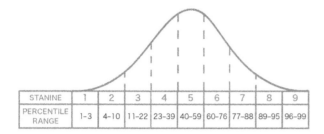

STANINE	1	2	3	4	5	6	7	8	9
PERCENTILE RANGE	1-3	4-10	11-22	23-39	40-59	60-76	77-88	89-95	96-99

Notice that the percentile ranges for the middle stanines of 4–6 are far larger than the ranges for the extreme stanines of 1, 2, 8, or 9. This means that most students taking the ISEE achieve scores in the middle ranges. Only the top 4% of all test takers receive a stanine of 9 on any given section, while 20% of students receive a stanine of 5.

So, what is a good ISEE score?

Stanine scores (which range from 1 to 9) are the most important and are the scores schools pay the most attention to. But what is a good score on the ISEE? A score of 5 or higher will be enough to put students in the running for most schools, although some elite private schools want applicants to have ISEE test results of 7 or higher.

Here's a sample ISEE Report

ISEE® INDEPENDENT SCHOOL ENTRANCE EXAM

Individual Student Report

Candidate for Grade	8
ID Number	
Gender	Male
Date of Birth	4/8/2004
Phone Number	
Test Level/Form	Middle/0916
Date of Testing	11/30/2016
Tracking Number	201612010592103

The Test Profile below shows your total scores for each test. Refer to the enclosed brochure called *Understanding the Individual Student Report* to help you interpret the *Test Profile* and *Analysis*. Percentile Ranks and Stanines are derived from norms for applicants to independent schools.

TEST PROFILE

Section	Scaled Score (760 – 940)	Percentile Rank (1 – 99)	Stanine (1 – 9)	Stanine Analysis
Verbal Reasoning	895	90	8	
Reading Comprehension	890	76	6	
Quantitative Reasoning	894	81	7	
Mathematics Achievement	883	61	6	

LEGEND: V = Verbal Reasoning R = Reading Comprehension Q = Quantitative Reasoning M = Mathematics Achievement

ANALYSIS

Section & Subsection	# of Questions	# Correct	Results for Each Question
Verbal Reasoning			
Synonyms	18	15	+++++++++- ++++- ++- +
Single Word Response	17	16	+++++++++++- +++++
Quantitative Reasoning			
Word Problems	18	11	+++- - - +++- +++++- - -
Quantitative Comparisons	14	14	++++++++++++++
Reading Comprehension			
Main Idea	4	4	++++
Supporting Ideas	6	5	- +++++
Inference	6	5	+- ++++
Vocabulary	7	5	+++- +- +
Organization/Logic	4	4	++++
Tone/Style/Figurative Language	3	3	+++
Mathematics Achievement			
Whole Numbers	7	4	+- +++- -
Decimals, Percents, Fractions	9	5	++- - ++- - +
Algebraic Concepts	11	7	+++++- ++- - -
Geometry	4	2	+- +-
Measurement	5	4	++++-
Data Analysis and Probability	6	4	+++- +-

LEGEND: + = Correct   - = Incorrect   S = Skipped   N = Not Reached

The test was administered in the order reported in the analysis section; Verbal Reasoning, Quantitative Reasoning, Reading Comprehension, and Mathematics Achievement. Each section was divided into subsections, grouping similar types of questions. The Reading Comprehension subsection grouping does not represent the actual order of the test questions.

The above is a preliminary ISEE report. ERB reserves the right to amend this report before it is finalized. The report will be final no later than 20 business days. The final report will automatically be generated electronically.

Ingram Content Group UK Ltd.
Milton Keynes UK
UKHW051810270623
423971UK00006B/42